SOLD IN SECRET

A mother's desperate search to find the men
who trafficked and killed her daughter

Karen Downes

with Joe and Ann Cusack

BLINK
bringing you closer

Published by Blink Publishing
2.25, The Plaza,
535 Kings Road,
Chelsea Harbour,
London, SW10 0SZ

www.blinkpublishing.co.uk

facebook.com/blinkpublishing
twitter.com/blinkpublishing

Paperback – 978-1-788-700-98-6
Ebook – 978-1-788-700-99-3

A CIP catalogue of this book is available from the British Library.

Designed and set by seagulls.net
Printed and bound in Great Britain by Clays Ltd, Elcograf S.p.A

1 3 5 7 9 10 8 6 4 2

Copyright © Karen Downes, 2018

Karen Downes has asserted her moral right to be identified as the author of this work in accordance with the Copyright, Designs and Patents Act 1988.

Every reasonable effort has been made to trace copyright holders of material reproduced in this book, but if any have been inadvertently overlooked the publishers would be glad to hear from them.

Blink Publishing is an imprint of Bonnier Books UK
www.bonnierbooks.co.uk

SOLD IN SECRET

To my beloved mum, children, grandchildren,
and all the other poor victims of grooming gangs.

CONTENTS

Prologue: May 2007   1

1: The Silk Shirt   5
2: Las Vegas of the North   22
3: Breaking Boundaries   39
4: Missing   49
5: A Silent Night   64
6: The Search   67
7: Who is Martina?   75
8: Unwelcome Attention   90
9: False Hope   99
10: Christmas Spirit   117
11: Wandering the Streets   123
12: Waiting by the Window   138
13: Psychic Visions   152
14: Sweet 16   157
15: A Breakthrough   161
16: An Empty Seat   170
17: Traded for a Bag of Chips   173

18: Media Feeding Frenzy   183

19: Shock Letter   190

20: Picking Up the Pieces   198

21: Stabbed in the Back   203

22: Homecoming   214

23: Moving House   231

24: A Desperate Mother   242

25: A New Love   251

26: Memorial Turmoil   263

27: The World Listens at Last   288

28: The Footage   295

Epilogue   302

Acknowledgements   312

PROLOGUE

MAY 2007

Trembling, I stood in the witness box. I could hardly breathe; I took a sip of water. My heart was thumping so hard, it felt like it would burst right out of my chest. Desperate to avoid all the eyes around me, I looked down at my feet. This was the first time I'd bought new shoes in years. Most mothers bought new clothes for celebrations – sweet-16- and 18th-birthday parties, weddings and big family occasions – but I had to buy a new outfit to look my best for my daughter's murder trial.

It was an odd thought, whirring round in my head, as the barristers shuffled their papers and a deathly hush fell. This was my day, the day I thought we would get justice. The world would hear about my little girl. I thought we would get the truth and perhaps some closure from the ongoing nightmare which had dominated our lives ever since our daughter had skipped out of our front door, four years ago, never to be seen again. I wanted an end to the misery of not knowing. The gnawing, sickening, agonising endless wait of not knowing.

The wait had weighed down on me; I was stooped, weary, cowed. This was my chance to fight back. One thing I felt sure of was that things couldn't get any worse, but I was wrong.

Today, the third day of the trial, was my chance to speak out. As arranged, a car had come at 8am to take me to court. The night before, I hadn't slept at all. I felt wired; wide awake, lying in Charlene's bed, surrounded by her teddies and her Darren Day and Westlife posters. I thought back to all the times she'd sung her heart out, hairbrush in hand, as she gazed at her idols on the wall. She was near, so near. I could smell her in the pillow. I heard her ghostly giggle in the stillness of the lonely hours before dawn. And she was far, so far. Almost as far away as I now was from myself.

The driver had played Kaiser Chiefs, at full volume, all the way to Preston Crown Court. It had seemed somehow inappropriate, disrespectful even.

'Ruby, Ruby, Ruby, Ruby!' screeched the radio.

And now, as I was beginning to recount my evidence to the court, I heard the same tune, over and over, grating and jarring, like a roadblock in my brain.

Come on, Karen, I steeled myself. *Don't let her down. Not now.*

I was her mother. She had just one mother – just one hope. And this was my time to be strong. I breathed again, I took another sip of water, and I swallowed the panic.

Reliving the day of Charlene's disappearance was in many ways like reading off a script. I had been over it so many times over the years, it no longer felt real.

I looked across at the two men in the dock. They stared straight ahead; they didn't even look at me.

Shouldn't they be made to look at me? I wondered. *Shouldn't they be made to answer my questions?*

I held a tatty little photo of Charlene in my hand. My mind drifted back; her kooky smile, her teenage back-chat and her trademark giggle. What I wouldn't give for one last cheeky broadside from her now …

I found I was suddenly ice-cold, shaking. I had come here for the truth, for justice, for a shred of comfort even, for my family. I wanted to stand up in court and scream. They didn't know her, none of them did. I was here to fight for my daughter. But how could I begin to confront this? I felt swamped, sickened, helpless.

Charlene was a child; a little girl. *My* little girl.

The last day we had together, she'd been singing along down her hairbrush to her Darren Day DVD. She'd had a tantrum over one lost trainer. And she had kissed me, put her arms around me and promised to be home safe.

Now her memory was being picked over by faceless, nameless men in wigs, like crows with a carcass. So fascinated by her death. So disinterested in her life.

CHAPTER ONE

THE SILK SHIRT

'Blackpool!' I announced, throwing my arms wide. 'What do you think?'

Our four children stared at me, taking in the news for a moment, before the little ones started whooping and jumping up and down.

'What, forever?' asked my second eldest daughter, Becki, the concept baffling her for a moment – as it had me.

I nodded and smiled. My husband Bob and I were both from Coventry; it was all we'd ever known. But now, it was time for a change. We hadn't been happy for a long time. I wanted something more, something different, something better, for my family.

Of course, it hadn't always been that way. Once upon a time, it had seemed that, as long as we had each other,

Bob and I could make anything happen. Naively, I had thought that if we loved each other, we would want the same things, make the same decisions, have the same goals. But as the years wore on, the traits I had once admired, or at least forgiven, became irritations.

If I was totally honest with myself, Bob wasn't the man I once thought. Or perhaps he was, but what I now wanted was different. And whether we'd both changed – or neither of us – seemed irrelevant, really. Bob didn't really talk about feelings and emotions and so I had absolutely no idea whether he thought the same about me. The fact was, we had four children, a life together, a past. And those shared memories of our family as it grew were enough to keep that bond strong. Each of our children's achievements and heartbreaks, which we felt even more keenly than they did, especially the heartbreaks, were imprinted on Bob and me like tattoos. I didn't want to let that go. And so I was practical enough to know that we needed to forge some sort of future together too.

* * *

I had been just 18 when we'd met at a rock and roll night at a local pub, The White Swan. Bob's satin shirt caught my eye straightaway as he gyrated on the dancefloor. He was quite the centre of attention and I felt myself blush as he smiled at me.

'Thinks he's Elvis,' my mum, Jessie, giggled. 'Look at those moves!'

She and I were best pals as well as mum and daughter so it wasn't unusual for us to have a Friday night out together. Sometimes, my nan, who was named Jessie too, came along – the women in our family were all close-knit. Dad had walked out when I was a baby and I very rarely saw him. Not that it troubled me much; Mum had enough love for the both of them. But as an only child, the thing I missed most was the company of brothers and sisters. I longed for noise and bustle, for arguments and cramped bedrooms, shared jokes and borrowed make-up.

Sunday mornings were spent at Sunday School, where Mum was a teacher. Sunday afternoons with Mum and Nan were lovely, watching old black-and-white films or maybe venturing out to the bingo. There was a club at the end of our road where you could go dancing on Saturdays, and children were allowed. So we'd both go along – Mum didn't like going anywhere without me. But what I wanted most was company my own age. Someone to giggle with. Someone to get into mischief with. Even a smack on the hand doesn't hurt so much if your partner in crime is getting one too. I used to line up my dollies in an old-fashioned coach pram and pretend they were my real babies – all ten or eleven of them.

'You'll make a smashing mum one day,' Mum used to say. 'I can imagine you with a big family, too.'

She was the perfect role model: warm, strong and unconditionally supportive. As a struggling single mum, she had no money, but she scrimped and saved so that I never went without. Our little flat was sparse, but clean and so homely. I was well loved, that was for sure.

I laughed along as she poked fun at Bob's dancing that night, but secretly, I was already bristling in his defence. I liked his shirt. And I could tell he liked me. It was as simple as that. When the record finished, he made a beeline for me and asked if he could buy me a drink.

'Don't mind if you do.' I smiled.

Truth was, I was on the rebound; my heart had been so recently broken and in my teenage world, it would take light years to mend. I'd been hopelessly infatuated with Lee, a boy I'd known since school. We'd gone out together for just a couple of months and I fell head over heels in love. But he was a flirt and a heartbreaker, and he had soon cleared off with one of my friends. Deep down, I'd been expecting it to happen, but the pain was sharp and raw all the same. And when I met Bob, I was still smarting. Yet in him, I could sense someone more reliable, settled, boring even. I could imagine him as the sort to put the bins out on time. To wire plugs, put up shelves, fall asleep in front of the telly. But that was exactly what I was looking for – I didn't want any more rollercoaster love. I looked at Bob and I could imagine a father, a husband, a homemaker.

'I'll be here next week,' I told him coyly. 'Wear that shirt.'

And so Bob and I began dating, or 'stepping out', as my mum called it. We met up the next week and the next, always at the rock and roll nights. And gradually, over 'Love Me Tender' and 'Jailhouse Rock', we fell in love. It wasn't the sort of whirlwind romance that gives you physical pain and makes you feel sick and giddy. I'd done that, and I didn't like it one bit. This was a steady, comforting type of love and I felt sure, above all, Bob wouldn't let me down. He was four years older than me; 22 when we met, and I liked that. It gave him a sense of worldliness and maturity. Mum had been right too: he was mad about Elvis. He could swing his hips along with the best of them and, as I watched him grind, week after week, I was glad he was mine.

As the weeks passed, Mum would let Bob stay over for weekends at our small, tidy council flat. He soon became part of the family; he was easy-going and full of jokes and quips, and Mum quickly warmed to him. We both loved dancing. Every weekend we went out, sometimes with a group of friends, other times on our own. We were just like any other young couple – we'd chat about the latest song in the charts, or bicker about whose turn it was to go to the bar. I didn't ask myself too many questions about why I was settling for him or what our future together might hold. I didn't really want the answers.

On February 2 1985, just over a year after we met, our eldest daughter, Emma, was born. A little over two years later, I proposed, and on May 2 1987, heavily pregnant and blooming, I married Bob. On June 9 that same year, we had a second daughter, Becki. By now, the nights out and the dancing were just a distant memory. The silk shirt gathered dust at the back of the wardrobe. But we had a new passion – our children. And Bob was a good dad. He wasn't expressive or affectionate in the same way as I was, but he worked hard and he was proud of his children. That was plain to see. And then, on March 25 1989, Charlene came along. At 8lb 6oz, she was a chubby, bouncing, gorgeous baby. I was a huge fan of the Australian soap, *Neighbours*, and so she was named after the character played by Kylie Minogue. My first choice of name was Kylie, but Bob wouldn't hear of it and so we settled on Charlene – I loved it. Her nickname was 'Babby', which suited her perfectly.

'You're my Babby,' I would tell her, kissing her nose. 'And you always will be.'

Unlike her sisters, Charlene was quite grizzly and demanding; she would scream the house down until she got her own way. She would wake three or four times a night and nothing could settle her.

'You've got me wrapped around your little finger,' I'd say, smiling as I cuddled her in the darkness of our bedroom.

But it got to the stage where I was dropping with exhaustion. Bob was working nights as a security guard, so I couldn't ask him to help out. Mum was still living with us, she had moved into our new flat to help out, so she would take the odd turn. And she would often get up too, just to keep me company, in those small hours on my own. But mostly, it was down to me – I was Charlene's mother, after all. And though I complained, half-heartedly, I secretly loved those precious moments, in the half-light, when the house was still and peaceful. I would gaze in wonder at her fat little cheeks, her fingers tightly wrapped around my thumb, her eyelashes resting on the smoothest of skin, and I would fall in love with her all over again. In those quiet hours, I'd daydream about the future, about who she might become and what she might do with her life.

'Be happy, darling,' I whispered, tucking her back into her cot. 'Be happy and be safe.'

As she grew into a toddler, Charlene became an adorable child. No longer whingey and whiney, she was adventurous and strong-willed. I'd hear her giggle as she tore around the house, carrying an armful of Emma and Becki's dolls, with them screaming in hot pursuit of her.

'You've got your own dollies,' I told her, waggling a finger and trying not to laugh.

But for Charlene, pinching theirs was half the fun. She had a streak of mischief that gave the house an energy all of its own. She loved climbing too. If there was a wall, she had to get over it. If she saw stairs, she'd take them two at a time. She would walk across the back of the sofa and the chairs or hang from the banisters.

'Get down!' I screamed. 'You'll break your neck!'

She was such a tomboy, not like her sisters at all. Becki and Emma liked a calming bedtime story before going to sleep, but Charlene was never one for sitting quietly and listening to stories – she preferred to sit in bed and have a good old-fashioned chat.

'She's like a little old woman,' Mum said. 'No wonder she and I are such good pals.'

* * *

In the Autumn of 1990, Bob and I rented a large, four-bed-roomed house in a quiet cul-de-sac, in a nice area of Coventry. It was the sort of street where Emma and Becki could play outside safely, wobbling along on their little bikes with me or Mum running behind. Mum had moved with us and she and Charlene shared a room. Poor Mum was often woken early by Charlene, lining up dollies and teddies on the bedroom carpet before it was even light, ready for yet another tea party.

Or they'd sing nursery rhymes, and swap jokes, underneath the quilt.

Mum even went along on a nursery school trip with her, to a farm outside the city. Charlene came home bursting with excitement because she'd fed a baby piglet all by herself.

'She's a natural.' Mum beamed. 'A little mummy in the making – just like you, Karen.'

One day, one of Emma's school friends named Erica came to play, and the kids all ran around together upstairs whilst I cooked tea. But then I heard a piercing shriek. I dropped my tea towel and dashed up the stairs to find Charlene, aghast, looking in the mirror – with most of her long, wavy light-brown hair on the carpet around her.

'Erica cut her hair, Mummy!' Emma announced.

And then she burst out laughing. Becki was roaring too. I had to admit, it was funny, but I kept my face straight. Poor Charlene looked like a monk. I took her to the hairdresser's that same night and she had to have a short back and sides. She wailed all the way home and I had to cuddle her to sleep that night.

'You must be exhausted,' Mum said when she peeped in on us.

I nodded, but it was a nice feeling. Charlene's face was pressed against my shoulder and I was sticky with snot and tears. But I didn't care one bit – I loved being a mum. And it certainly seemed that motherhood was for me. I fell pregnant again, and our son, Robert, was born on June 29 1991. Like his sisters, he was beautiful; perfect. We nicknamed him 'Trebor' because it was Robert backwards. One day, Emma was reading his name out from one of the baby cards and for some reason, she read it out backwards too. We all laughed and the name stuck. He was a funny, cute little boy, adored and spoilt by his big sisters. I felt blessed – our family was complete, and this was all I had ever wanted.

Bob and I had our differences when it came to dealing with the children but it was to be expected, I told myself. He had always been a very straightforward, inflexible sort of man. At bedtimes, if the children were misbehaving, he would shout and swear and frighten them up the stairs to bed. Minutes later, they'd be tucked up in bed alright – but shaking and sobbing. I couldn't stand it. Creeping in to comfort them, I knew I was risking his wrath. And sure enough, a few minutes later, his voice thundered up the stairs.

'Don't undermine me,' he shouted. 'I can discipline my own children, I don't need your help.'

There was no reasoning with Bob. For him, situations were black or white, whereas I could always find a shade of grey. I didn't like him shouting at the children, but I also knew it caused even more trouble when I confronted him. Once or twice he would raise his fist towards me and I shrank back in alarm. There was so little affection between us. I couldn't remember the last time we'd had a laugh – a real good laugh – together. *These days, I was more likely to get a clip round the ear off him than a kiss*, I thought bitterly.

Mum could see what was happening and she offered to babysit: 'It will do you both good, Karen,' she said quietly, pressing a £10 note into my hand.

We went for a drink at the local pub and I'd been hoping we could talk and reconnect a little, but Bob spotted a couple of his pals and went off to play snooker in the next room. I was left with my lonely vodka, still nursing a bruise under my eye from our last argument, and I grew angry and bitter. I wasn't used to putting myself first, not with four children. But it seemed Bob had never lost the habit. I was 27 years old, but I felt that life was passing me by; I wanted to grab that last slice of youth before it dissolved in my hands. Perhaps I was unhappy with Bob, and perhaps I was unhappy with myself. And so it was that I began drifting away from my marriage; mentally at first, but then the rest logically followed. Through friends I met a man called Terry. Like me, he was unhappily married and we were both looking for an escape, a reminder that life could still be fun. I recognised the way Terry looked at me. And I liked it.

'Meet me one night,' he pleaded.

It wasn't easy – I had the children to think of. I felt shameful too, lying to everyone. But a part of me was reckless, clawing back some youth, maybe, before it was too late. Terry and I both knew that it was no more than a fling.

Just one month in, Bob confronted me, eyes blazing, and I panicked.

'You're having an affair!' he shouted. 'I know all about it, Karen.'

Trembling, I tried to defend myself, to explain how unhappy I was – how lonely I felt. But Bob was raging. That night, I slept on the couch. Bob hadn't calmed down at all by the next morning.

'I'm moving out,' he announced.

And in a way, though I was ashamed to admit it, I felt a sense of relief. Perhaps this was best for us all. He arranged to stay with his mum but not before I had packed him some clothes, a toothbrush and pyjamas in a supermarket carrier bag. Even now, I was mothering him, looking after him.

What kind of wife packs a bag for their husband when they're walking out? I wondered.

At first, I didn't miss him one bit. The children and I did just as we liked – it was almost as though we were on holiday. I bought them chips, they stayed up late, we watched films ... I frittered money away on treats, without much thought of how I'd cope in the long term. Truth was, I didn't want to think about the future at all. Deep down, I hoped it would all work out, somehow. And the holiday period grew stale, inevitably. Chips every night are no longer a treat.

'He's their dad, and he's your husband,' Mum reminded me. 'There's a lot at stake here.'

Mum didn't want to see me upset. She hated to see me hurt. But she'd struggled as a single mum herself and she didn't want that for me. The children missed their dad, and begrudgingly, I had to admit I did too. It was the silly things, like hearing him swearing to himself as he fell over the kids' shoes by the door when he came in from work. Or him hogging the bathroom in the mornings when I was dying for the loo. I missed the smell of him, too, especially in bed. I would hold his pillow close and think back to how happy we'd once been. So, when he knocked on the door, shifting uneasily from one foot to the other on the doorstep, I was pleased.

'Can I come in?' he asked.

I nodded. He popped in the next day and the next. I felt myself softening.

'I can't live without you, Karen,' he blurted out one day. 'I will kill myself if I lose my family.'

It wasn't like Bob to make such a statement. I knew he

was serious. And so, I agreed to a reconciliation. We had been apart for eight months.

'Another chance,' I said and nodded.

And I felt better when he came back: our family was back together and that was important to me. Mum smiled and welcomed him back. But there was a steeliness in her eyes and I knew she was watching every move he made. She was wise enough not to step in to our squabbles, not unless she absolutely had to. But I knew, unconditionally, that she was there for me. She was the one person who would always be on my side.

'Men are a difficult breed,' she would sigh.

And I had to agree. Sometimes, I would look at Bob and wonder ... Was it loyalty, sympathy or just habit that was keeping us together? I didn't really know. It certainly wasn't passion or undying love. But I resolved to try and scratch along with him as best I could. As the years passed, there were more niggles and more fractures in our relationship. We argued mostly over the children. I was too soft, Bob said; he was too harsh, I'd reply. And with each incident, I felt myself sail a little further away from him. But I said nothing. Bob wouldn't have understood or wanted to understand either. In many ways, I told myself, I was a typical married woman: I had settled for this man, and now I had to make the best of it.

* * *

When Charlene was four, we took her on her first holiday to Blackpool. We stayed in a little B&B overlooking the seafront, and every morning, the kids would scramble into their shorts and T-shirts before heading off onto the beach.

They didn't care if it rained, they were out there regardless – building sandcastles, chasing seagulls, with their hoods up and their wellies on. Emma and Becki would paddle at the edge of the water, screaming partly with laughter and partly with cold, as they splashed each other. Becki was most definitely the ringleader; persuading Emma into the water, leading her into mischief. Becki was the boss of the entire family really – she could marshal us all around like willing troops. Little Robert was a typical boy; if he wasn't dribbling a football along the firmer sand near the shore, he'd be filling his pockets with sand or stones, or dead crabs.

'Look, Mummy, this one is asleep,' he told me.

Charlene adored animals from an early age and she would set off down the beach at full pelt, her hair streaming in the wind, towards the line of waiting donkeys.

'Can I have a ride, Mummy?' she begged. 'Please? I like the brown one. He has such sad eyes, Mummy.'

Just watching the children made me feel content, as though I was getting something right, as a mum. I loved the air in Blackpool too; fresh and clean, so that you could fill the very bottom of your lungs with it. I felt sure it was good for the children – it had to be. In the evenings, we walked along the North Pier, gazing at the gaudy stalls and the neon signs and listening to the endless chink chink of the slot machines. It was bamboozling for the senses; my own head was swimming. The children's faces lit up against all the coloured lights, their faces shining in fluorescent wonder.

'Can we live here forever?' Charlene pleaded. 'I love it, Mummy!'

We went back on holiday, every summer, and each was as idyllic as the last. We went to the top of the Tower and looked out giddily across the sea. We went on fair rides and to the waxwork museum. And we came home laden with sea shells, sticky rock and candyfloss. We couldn't afford to go abroad, but the children never wanted to – we had so much fun in Blackpool. One summer, when Charlene was seven years old, my mum had taken the children out to the arcade and whilst they were there, Charlene, ever devoted to animals, had spotted a dog and had run over to stroke it. But it had snapped and bitten her hand, and when Mum came rushing back to our B&B, Charlene was sobbing, her hand wrapped in one of Mum's hankies.

'We need to get her to hospital,' I said anxiously.

We soon found ourselves in A&E at Blackpool Victoria, but even as we waited in the queue, Charlene was brightening up.

'It was a nice dog, Mummy,' she told me. 'It didn't mean to hurt me.'

Her injuries, thankfully, weren't serious and she was allowed home with dressings. The dog's owner had left the arcade without so much as an apology and Bob hit the roof when Mum told him.

'Oh, I'd give her a piece of my mind!' he fumed.

But even Bob couldn't stay angry in Blackpool for long. We went back the next year, and even the hospital trip seemed like a fond memory now. Blackpool had a way of just turning things around, as though a little bit of the sparkle from the Illuminations was shining on us as well. Bob and I got on better there too – it was as if we left the old cracked shell of our relationship back in Coventry and we could take a break from our list of gripes for a while.

CHAPTER TWO

LAS VEGAS OF THE NORTH

Late one night, the kids were all in bed and Bob was at work on a night shift. I was busy making me and Mum a last brew before we turned in, but as I poured in the milk, the front door slammed and I heard Bob swearing under his breath. Instantly, my heart sank. I ran into the hallway. There were blotchy, angry patches across his face and his knuckles were clenched white. I could guess immediately what had happened.

'You've been sacked, haven't you?' I said quietly, hoping against hope I was wrong.

Bob spat out something about the boss being a fool. His tirade was peppered with swear words and mutterings, but I got the general idea and my heart sank. He had lost his temper, he'd told the boss to 'Fuck off' and that was that.

'Bob, what are we going to do?' I asked, my voice cracking in despair. 'Did you even think about us when you were giving him a piece of your mind? Did you think about the rent or the food bills, or the kids' school shoes?'

As the reality hit me, the tears sprang from my eyes. Bob hadn't ever learned to keep his mouth shut. All it had taken was one wrong word from his boss and he had exploded with rage. It hadn't mattered to him that he had a family and a wife to look after. All that had mattered was him having his say, making his point. And now, we had no income. No money. Nothing.

'Well, I hope it was worth it,' I said, anger rising. 'You're top dog now, Bob, aren't you? You've made your point, so well done!'

My tone was thick with sarcasm but I didn't care. Normally, speaking like this to Bob would have been going too far and I knew it. He would have turned on me next. But he could sense my disappointment, my desperation.

'We'll manage,' he replied stiffly. 'I'll think of something.'

It was beyond him to apologise, I knew that through bitter experience. But I knew also that he realised what a mess he'd made: we had four little children to look after. It was a frightening prospect and that night, I lay awake, anxiously running through a mental checklist of all the things we had to pay for.

Bob went out first thing the next day, and the next. He tried hard to get another job, but it wasn't so easy, having been sacked from the last one. We had a beautiful big home, a private rent, in a nice area of Coventry. But we just couldn't afford it without Bob's wage. I didn't smoke or drink; I never spent a penny on myself and I just couldn't see where the savings could be made. Instead, I made jam sandwiches for the kids' teas and sent them to bed early each night to save on heating. I went without meals myself to the point where I felt so empty inside that I was dizzy and disorientated. I felt hopeless, an utter failure. Mum, kind-hearted as ever, helped where she could with her pension money, but it wasn't enough. I sobbed when, six months on, our eviction notice dropped through the letterbox. I felt like we'd let the children down. And, of course, we had.

Wearily, we packed up and moved to emergency council accommodation on a rough estate. Mum came too and she couldn't help wrinkling her nose in disgust when she saw the state of the kitchen, thick with years of second and third-hand grease. But it was all they could offer us.

'We'll be fine,' I assured the kids, smiling through gritted teeth as they ran around the new house. Their shoes on the bare floorboards jarred my already pounding headache.

They ran off to explore, but they had only been out playing for a few minutes when a strange woman knocked on the door and accused Charlene of stealing jewellery from her.

'She took my necklace and she dropped it down a grid,' spat the woman.

'I don't think so,' I said politely.

But the woman became aggressive, jabbing her finger in my face and demanding money to pay for her missing necklace. I was terrified; I didn't know what to do.

'I'll pay you back,' I promised eventually, my voice quivering.

I knew full well Charlene hadn't stolen anything – she was only seven years old and she was a good girl. But it seemed the best way to get rid of the woman, off the doorstep.

When Bob came home, he was predictably furious.

'Please don't make things worse,' I pleaded.

But he was already pulling on his boots and marching out into the street, bawling at the top of his voice.

'I won't have my family treated like that,' he yelled, banging on the woman's door.

I burst into tears. This wasn't helping at all. In the past, maybe, I'd have been proud of Bob, standing up for his family, taking no nonsense from bullies. Now, I just wanted him to keep his mouth shut. I watched through the smears on our filthy living-room window as he and the woman shouted and screamed for a few minutes and then she slammed the door in his face. But I feared this was just the start of it.

And in the weeks afterwards, local kids threw stones and bricks at the house. Our windows were smashed and there was rubbish chucked over the fence, strewn across the garden. The kids were too afraid to play out. And I didn't really want them out of my sight either. There were druggies and drinkers hanging around, right at the end of our street. I was too scared to walk past them, with my shopping, in case I was attacked or mugged. Their language was disgusting – I was no prude, and I liked to think I had compassion for other people, but I couldn't live like this.

'We don't fit in here,' I said to Bob. 'I hate it.'

I carried on, day to day. I had no choice. I tried to make myself defiant and hard; I would set my jaw aggressively like the other women I saw. But it just wasn't me. Inside, I was shaking.

Part of me blamed Bob, for losing his job. I wanted him to get us out of the mess he'd created. Yet if someone shouted at him, he would just shout back – even louder. He didn't let the street bother him the same way I did. But for me, it was hell, as I dreaded confrontation and, more than anything, I hated the way our children had been dumped right in the middle of it all. I applied for a move, out of the area, because I just wanted to get away. Two months on, we were given a house in Walsall. It was miles away from everything we knew, but I was desperate. And yet, the next house, on a grey, damp little street, was hardly any better. Mum sighed in exasperation as we carried in our belongings.

'Now I thought the last kitchen was bad!' she spluttered.

And Bob fell out with the neighbours before we'd even unpacked. One man complained that our van had taken up his parking space and for Bob, that was all it took. I saw his jaw twitch and my heart sank.

'I'm moving house!' he yelled. 'Keep your mouth shut, you bloody idiot!'

It seemed as though he couldn't stop arguing – he was always so angry.

'What's wrong with you?' I snapped. 'Why can't you get along with people?'

'It's not me, it's them,' he insisted.

And I realised I was wasting my breath. Even so, I had a bad feeling about the street. That same week, I pegged my washing out and someone set the line on fire. Our clothes were ruined. People would come right up to the window and peer inside our house. I felt like I was living in a zoo.

'What are we going to do?' I asked Bob wearily. 'I want better than this for the kids.'

He turned to me and smiled – and for a moment I had a glimpse of the satin shirt and the swinging hips I'd fallen in love with.

'What about Blackpool, Las Vegas of the North?' he said. 'I think we'd be happy there.'

I stared.

'Not a holiday, Bob,' I replied. 'I'm talking about somewhere to live.'

He nodded.

'So am I.' He grinned. 'I think it would be perfect.'

At first, I dismissed the idea completely. It seemed crazy, moving our whole family over 100 miles north. We knew nobody in Blackpool, we had no reason at all to go there. Yet I couldn't deny we'd always had such happy times there; we'd always felt at home.

'Why Blackpool?' Mum asked suspiciously, when she heard.

'Why *not* Blackpool?' Bob quipped.

And I had to admit, he had a point. Mum laughed too.

'I do love the Tower,' she conceded. 'And the sea air would be good for my arthritis.'

Bob was keen. He started looking for houses to rent, making phone calls, filling out forms. It seemed like he couldn't wait to move. And I was really starting to love the idea. I thought back over the happy memories we had of the penny arcades and the beach. The kids loved it. And I realised Bob was absolutely right. I began to feel strongly – almost instinctively – that Blackpool was the place for us. It was so obvious, I didn't know how I'd missed it for so long. Even so, breaking the news to the children, over breakfast one morning, my stomach was turning over, a fizzy mixture of apprehension and excitement. I could feel myself starting to giggle (which was just like Charlene when she was nervous too).

'Blackpool!' Emma shrieked, throwing down her toast in disgust. 'You must be joking!'

At 14, she'd just met her first serious boyfriend and was horrified at the thought of leaving him.

'I know it's hard, but there's a whole new life waiting for us,' I promised her. 'Let's do it, whilst you're young. Blackpool is full of nice young men.'

Emma wasn't convinced. She abandoned her breakfast and marched off to her room to sulk. But I wasn't too concerned. It was just a teenage romance and she would soon bounce back.

The other three were thrilled. They couldn't quite grasp the idea that we were going for good. Charlene, in particular, was over the moon. Now ten years old, she was brimming with enthusiasm and mischief, and she thought living in Blackpool would be one long holiday.

'It won't be donkey rides and ice creams every day,' I reminded her. But the thought of living by the sea was exciting, for us all.

'Las Vegas of the North,' Bob said again. 'That's Blackpool for you.'

Two weeks on, and he had signed up for a furnished house, right on the seafront, and it was perfect for us. We applied for housing benefit, just until we got sorted with jobs. Everything was slotting into place. Mum and I began packing boxes, folding clothes into suitcases, wrapping pots in newspapers. Bob had a friend with a big van and he agreed to help us move.

'Can I have my own donkey?' Charlene asked, jumping up and down as I taped up yet another box.

'Can we give it a name?' Robert wanted to know.

I laughed. It was great to see them all looking forward to something. Even Emma agreed, despite herself, that she was looking forward to living next door to the Pleasure Beach.

'I'll need extra pocket money,' she bargained with a teenage scowl. 'There's a lot to buy in Blackpool.'

'Agreed.' I grinned.

I'd have agreed to anything at all, right at that moment. It felt so good that we were *doing* something, taking control of our lives. At last. The kids sang all the way to Blackpool. Britney Spears and Boyzone blasted out of the radio. And then Westlife came on and the three girls went wild. Emma and Becki loved Westlife and Charlene copied them because it was the cool thing to do. It really felt as though we were off on the most exciting trip of our lives – it might as well have been Las Vegas. And as we pulled up outside our new home, I inhaled a lungful of salty air, mixed with smells of candyfloss and cockles, and I felt a rush of happiness. The seagulls squawked a scruffy welcome as they divebombed in the distance.

'Watch those seagulls, they'll take your ice creams out of your hands, given half a chance,' Bob said, and the kids giggled.

I smiled too. Even the threat of a delinquent seagull couldn't dampen our day. Mum scurried off to the chip shop to buy lunch, and Bob and I began unloading. By the afternoon, the kids were so loud and restless that he gave in and agreed to take them down to the beach. We were only a ten-minute walk away from the sea; we could smell the salt from the front door and it was irresistible. By the time they tramped back home, the light was fading and they had sand in their shoes and their pockets were crammed with shells, pebbles and the odd crab's leg. I had unpacked enough to make up the beds and find pyjamas for us all. That night, they slept so soundly, and I did too: I felt this was where we belonged.

The next morning, we were woken by seagulls and the noise of traders opening up stalls on the promenade.

'Can we go to the pier?' Charlene begged. 'Come on, Mummy!'

I hadn't finished unpacking and the house was in chaos, but it was a wonderfully warm Saturday morning in July, the start of the school holidays too, and weather like this was too good to waste. Hastily, I emptied what coppers I could find in my purse and I set off, hand in hand with Charlene and Robert, with Emma and Becki behind. Though it was mid-morning, the pier was already bustling with life. The kids ran off, clattering down the wooden planks towards the penny arcades, screaming with delight at a clown on stilts who came striding past. After the stagnation of our old life, the claustrophobic condensation of joyless Coventry, Blackpool felt like a burst of colour, energy and life. I went home feeling like I could take on the world.

'Won't be hard to get a job here,' I said to Bob, as I threw bacon in the pan for breakfast.

I had softened towards him; I could feel it. He had worked so hard to make the move happen. And though usually not at all affectionate, he slipped his arm around me and gave me a kiss.

'Must be the sea air,' I laughed.

We didn't have deep, emotional talks about our relationship, about rocky patches and fresh starts and the like – that just wasn't Bob at all. With him, it was best left unsaid. But I hoped to myself that perhaps Blackpool was a new beginning, in every sense, for us all.

And it seemed I was right. In less than two weeks, Bob had found a job as a doorman. It was long, late hours, but it paid well. And it turned out he had a cousin, Maureen, in Blackpool, who helped me find work in a hotel, just for the rest of the season. It was ideal. We got the children into schools and they seemed to settle in straightaway. Charlene made lots of friends, and next door she came across a little boy called Martin, who she instantly latched on to. Martin had moved into the street the day before us so they were like two little lost sheep huddling together and soon became inseparable. I would see them walking hand in hand, down the street, chatting away like a couple of pensioners. Martin had an old-fashioned outlook on life, just like Charlene. She nicknamed him 'Gilbert' for some quirky reason and it stuck.

'He looks like a "Gilbert",' she giggled. 'It's cute.'

A few weeks later, she bounded into the house with Martin and said: 'Can we go to Sunday School?'

I laughed in surprise. Though I had a strong faith, I wasn't a regular churchgoer – none of us went to church. But Mum was very religious and of course she had been a Sunday School teacher when she was younger so it seemed very fitting for Charlene to follow in her footsteps, with them being so close.

'What makes you want to go to Sunday School?' I asked curiously.

It turned out Charlene had met one of the Salvation Army teachers on the street outside our house. Her name was Carol and she was pushing an old-fashioned pram.

'I went over to look at her baby,' Charlene told me, a smile playing round the corners of her mouth. 'But instead there was a dog sitting in the pram, covered in blankets!'

She and Martin burst into peals of laughter at the memory.

'The dog is too old to go for walks,' Charlene explained. 'So he sits in the pram!'

Carol knocked on our door later that week to introduce herself. She was a lovely, kind woman and I could see why Charlene had taken to her. From then on, each week without fail, Charlene and Martin went to Sunday School. The church was just at the end of our street and I could watch them coming and going, gossiping away, fingers entwined, their faces so carefree it almost broke my heart.

'It's working out so well,' I would say, half-congratulating myself. 'This is the best move we ever made.'

Bob and I were getting on fine too. He was busy at work, and I was so glad we had a steady income at last and some stability for the children. If I was honest, I quite liked him being out of the house every night until 3 or 4am – Mum and I could enjoy a cup of tea and a natter in peace.

'I get on so much better with Bob when he's not here,' I told her and we both burst into giggles.

On his nights off, we even had the odd evening out. Bob's family came to visit from Coventry and we went out for a meal and drinks. We liked the British Legion club in Fleetwood, because we could dance in there. I found myself laughing with him once more and really having fun. It was as though this little house in Blackpool had taught us all how to enjoy life again. Of course, it was no palace; though it had four bedrooms, the rooms were smaller and so it was cramped and there was no privacy and no peace. But then, that was what I had always dreamed of – a big family around me. Charlene still shared a bedroom with my mum, but she didn't mind. Even though she was getting older, the two of them were as close as ever. We had no garden, just a backyard, and it was cluttered with bins and the kids' bikes. But in this house, with the windows flung open, you could taste the smell of the sea – and that was magical!

After the hotel work came to an end, I got another little job, this time handing out leaflets for a local Indian take-away restaurant on the seafront. Mum would look after the kids whilst I was working. It wasn't the most glamor-ous job; I'd get drunken hen parties who threw the leaflets back in my face, or groups of middle-aged men, leering as they passed. It didn't pay much either, but it allowed us a few luxuries – the odd Chinese takeaway or fish and chips on Saturday nights – after I'd been paid. Charlene's favourite treat was a chippy tea. If I was flush, I'd take the girls down to the promenade to buy them clothes and bits of make-up and jewellery. Though Charlene was too young for make-up, she was mad on collecting teddy bears and cassette tapes. We'd come home, triumphant, with a bagful of bargains.

'All tat,' Bob snorted dismissively. 'Useless rubbish.'

'Exactly.' I beamed. 'That's the whole idea.'

Whilst I caught up on housework on Sundays, Bob took the kids down to the beach for a ride on the donkeys.

'We gave them Polo mints and they ate the lot!' Charlene told me excitedly. 'Dad says donkeys love them.'

On rainy weekends, he took them into the arcades, pushing coppers into the penny drop machines. The kids lost more than they won, every week, yet came home victorious.

'We're in Las Vegas, just like Dad said,' Charlene reminded us.

At the end of the summer, the Illuminations began and the kids were thrilled. People would drive from far and wide to see the famous lights – and all *we* had to do was walk to the end of our street.

'We're so lucky!' Charlene exclaimed. 'We live in the middle of all the fun, don't we?'

I laughed and nodded. She had hit the nail right on the head.

* * *

Charlene was bright and she was doing so well at school. Hard-working and well behaved, she also took her faith very seriously and never missed Sunday School, always with Martin in tow. She was even picked to perform a solo in the school Nativity.

'"Silent Night" – in German!' she said proudly.

The tears trickled down my cheeks as I sat in the audience, listening to her sing. By the following September, when Charlene went to high school, she was singing and dancing all the time, twirling around the living room with a hairbrush, swooning over Darren Day and Westlife. One day, she burst in from school, whooping with breathless excitement.

'Darren Day is coming to Blackpool!' she announced grandly. She thumped the dining table hard for emphasis. 'I could bump into him!' she babbled. 'Can I have a day off school, wait outside the theatre?'

Her mind was working at a million miles an hour.

'We'll save up for tickets,' I promised, as Bob groaned.

All too predictably, two weeks later, I found myself standing at the stage door, in the rain, waiting for Charlene's teenage crush to emerge. When she spotted Darren Day, she got so giddy, I thought she was going to faint.

'I can't believe he's real,' she breathed. '*Is* he real, Mum?'

I had to swallow my giggles so as not to offend her. For Charlene, this was true love: she had lost her heart completely to Darren Day. Of course, the next morning, she and Martin skipped off to Sunday School, hand in hand, as usual. Darren Day was now a dream, and she was happy for him to stay that way. Later in the year, I bought tickets for us all to see him perform in *Summer Holiday* at the Winter Gardens Theatre. It was Mum's birthday and we took her out for a meal before the show. Through the gloom in the theatre, I caught her swooning over Darren Day – just like Charlene.

'You're as bad as each other,' I laughed, shaking my head. 'We should form a fan club.'

By the end of the summer, we'd met Darren Day so many times I had even got to know some of the other mums in the stage-door queue. Charlene collected all sorts of signed memorabilia, which she treasured above all else.

'We should invite Darren Day round for tea,' Bob said drily. 'He's like a member of the family.'

I wasn't sorry when the show's run came to an end and my evenings in the rain were over. But the memory of Charlene's face, shining with damp happiness, would live with me forever. Those snapshot moments of her bright sunrise smile in the rain at the stage door seemed trivial at the time – I had no idea that soon those golden memories would be all I had left.

CHAPTER THREE

BREAKING BOUNDARIES

The next few years went like a dream – Bob in a steady job, the kids doing well at school, and everyone still loving the escape that Blackpool was for us. Three years on, in 2003, Emma had just turned 18, Becki was 16, Robert was 12 and Charlene was 14. She had become a bit of a handful lately and her behaviour began to unravel. At home, she was answering back, giving cheek, laughing at my rules. When she went out, I didn't know where she was, or who she was with. Bob's way of dealing with her was to shout and lay down the law – just as he did with everyone else. But that didn't work with Charlene. And mum didn't fret too much about it. She and Charlene were so close, she hated to see anything bad in her, and she just felt it was a phase.

Charlene's behaviour had all started really with her older sister, Becki. Emma was a dream; she was good at school, well behaved and polite. I had no problems ever with her. Robert was a good lad too; a handful tearing around the house, chipping the paintwork with his football, but just a typical little boy. Then, quite out of the blue – and for no reason I could fathom – Becki began refusing to wear her school uniform.

'It's horrible!' she whined. 'I'm not wearing it and that's that.'

'Well, you're not allowed in school without your uniform!' I said in exasperation.

'Fine by me,' Becki quipped.

She stationed herself on the sofa, shielded by a duvet, TV remote in one hand, a bag of crisps in the other.

'That's not a healthy breakfast for a start,' I said.

But I soon realised the crisps were the least of my problems; 9am came and went, and she didn't seem in the least bit bothered.

'Go to school, Becki, please,' I pleaded.

But she just rolled her eyes and told me, in no uncertain terms, to clear off. It was a stalemate. Bob got involved, heavy-handed, shouting and bawling at her. But Becki was more than a match for him. Now a stroppy teenager, brimming with defiant hormones, she was ready for war. No longer did she scamper for cover at the sound of her dad's temper.

'F*** off, Dad!' she shouted. 'Just f*** off!'

I was flabbergasted – I'd never heard her swear like that. But it was a taste of things to come. Next, her teacher called and told me she was misbehaving in class, arriving late – and sometimes not at all.

'I'm sorry,' I said wearily. 'I'm doing my best with her.'

A few days later, I found her black school skirt under her bed, cut into ribbons.

'That settles it,' she smirked. 'I can't go in now, can I?'

I was horrified; she wasn't in the least bit sorry. If nothing else, it was a complete waste of a good uniform.

'They're not cheap, you know,' I shouted angrily. 'Money doesn't grow on bloody trees.'

In my frustration, I started to cry. Perhaps a small part of me thought that Becki might soften if she realised how upset I was. But like most teenagers, she seized on the smallest sign of weakness and began to laugh. I knew she didn't mean it, but that didn't make it any easier. So I called school and the Education Department came to see us at home.

'This can't carry on, Becki,' said the welfare officer.

Becki sulked and moaned and eventually agreed that she would be at school the following day. But she had been too easily talked round and I knew there was little hope of the truce lasting for long. Days later, the school called to say she was playing truant again.

'But she leaves for school,' I insisted. 'I put her on the bus myself.'

What I didn't know – until I grilled Becki – was that she was getting off the bus two stops down and going off shopping for the day, using her pocket money or a weekly £5 treat from my mum. Even when we stopped her spends, she would just window-shop. Nothing I said, or did, seemed to make any difference at all. Bob ranted and raved; he and I rowed. It was wearying, day after day. I felt like I was failing as a mum and it was the worst feeling – I didn't mind not being the best cook or forgetting to pay a gas bill, but I wanted to be a good mum.

'I don't know what to do with you,' I told Becki sadly.

The Education Authority evidently didn't know either. They eventually agreed on a compromise with Becki. She was sent to a specialist centre to finish her education, where there was no uniform, but she had to promise to attend every day.

'Done,' she agreed.

She stuck to her word and she loved the new centre. But for me, as a mother, there was hardly a sense of achievement. It wasn't what I wanted for my children. One afternoon, I was out on a bargain hunt, round the local charity shops, and I spotted an advert in the window of Barnardo's for a parenting course. Well, it couldn't do any harm, that was for sure. I went home and showed Bob the details, but he snorted scornfully and said, 'I don't need some bloody do-gooders telling me how to raise my own kids, Karen.'

His response was expected and disappointing in equal measure. And so I went along on my own. Nervous at first, I needn't have been: it was a real eye-opener. The tutors were genuine and caring, their ideas brilliantly simple.

'Talk to your children,' I was told. 'And listen to them too. Set boundaries. Be consistent. Explain everything.'

I loved it. And I felt like I was doing something, addressing my problems. I had that same feeling as when we'd arrived in Blackpool – I was taking life by the scruff of the neck. And so I switched off the TV and chatted to the kids. I set rules for bedtimes and homework. And then, just as I felt I was making progress, it started with Charlene.

'I want to go to the centre with Becki,' she moaned. 'I don't like wearing a uniform, I don't like school.'

Charlene looked up to Becki and she copied everything her big sister did, so I suppose I should have seen this coming. But it was still a blow, like going in for Round Two – with the bruises from Round One still smarting.

'You're going to school, and that's that,' I told Charlene firmly.

But, just like Becki, she thought she knew best.

'I only need to misbehave and then I'll get into the centre with Becki,' she said smugly.

It was all a game to Charlene, but then, with some experience behind me and the parenting course too, I felt more confident this time around. I was well used to dealing with teenagers so I wasn't worried, more frustrated. Next, Charlene began playing truant, taking the odd day off with Becki, to go shopping. And she was caught smoking in the Asda toilets too, just opposite the school. I didn't smoke, and neither did Bob. I was disgusted. The Polo mints she'd once fed to the donkeys now became her feeble attempt at masking the smoke smells, but they didn't work with me: she stank of smoke.

'It's vile and it has to stop,' I told her, throwing her entire outfit into the wash pile. 'You've gone too far.

'Anyway, where are you getting the money to buy cigarettes?'

Charlene smirked and marched off to her bedroom. The door slammed, the house shook slightly and a dusting of loose plaster fell from the doorframe. I sighed. She was hard work – and getting harder.

Sure enough, she got her own way and she was excluded from school for smoking. She was offered a place at the same centre where Becki was, and though the two girls whooped for joy, for me it was another hollow victory. But what bothered me most wasn't the bad behaviour. In some ways, I felt as though Charlene – like Becki – was slowly growing away from me. At just 14, she seemed to be shutting me out. We'd always shared a strong bond, yet these days she didn't really talk to me any more. It seemed like it was one argument after another. I didn't know where she was going when she bunked off school, or how she paid for her cigarettes and her bus fares, but every time I tried to ask, we ended up arguing. And I hated that. More than anything, I wanted us to be friends again. Instead, she began confiding in my mum. They were two of a kind and they always had been. They still shared a bedroom and late at night, just recently, I'd heard them giggling and whispering through the wall. I was glad, of course, that Charlene was at least talking to someone in the family, but I had to admit a small part of me was jealous too – I felt pushed out.

'I think Charlene has a urine infection,' Mum told me one morning. 'She's been complaining of pain when she goes to the loo.'

I was taken aback – Charlene hadn't mentioned it.

'Probably too embarrassed,' Mum reassured me.

I nodded. We saw the GP and got antibiotics. He didn't seem to think it was anything to worry about.

Soon after, Mum found me and said: 'Charlene has started her period, I thought you should know.'

Shocked, I said nothing.

'At least she's talking to one of us.' Mum smiled. 'Don't worry, Karen, she'll come round.'

But it stung. Were we so far apart that Charlene couldn't even tell me she was growing into a woman? I wondered what else she wouldn't – or couldn't – tell me.

She was staying out later too – later than she was allowed – hanging around the penny arcades.

'I won't have it!' Bob yelled, standing between her and the door one night. 'You're not going out looking like that!'

It was a stand-off. But unlike Becki, Charlene didn't enjoy a head-on row, preferring instead to swerve the collision. She merely smirked and quipped: 'Whatever you say, Sergeant Major.'

She changed and skipped out of the house wearing her jeans and trainers. But I knew her shoulder bag was stuffed with contraband clothes and make-up. I said nothing to Bob – it would only make things worse. The thing was, Charlene was a tomboy. I knew, deep down, she would much rather be at home in her tracksuit, watching her Darren Day DVDs. She was experimenting – pushing the boundaries – playing at being a grown-up.

'It's just a phase,' I told Bob, weary with enforced patience. 'If you stop her doing it, she'll rebel even more. Let her get it out of her system.'

But he had his way of handling her and I had mine. We clashed with each other just as we clashed with Charlene; it was exhausting. But again, it was just a part of parenting. I wasn't overly anxious because although Charlene was a challenge, she also loved Sunday School and cuddling up with her nanna in bed. She was still my little 'Babby' at heart. Not long before, I'd asked her to nip to the postbox for me and I'd handed her the letter and the money for a stamp.

'Stop at the newsagent's on your way,' I said to her. 'They sell stamps there.'

Half an hour later, she arrived home and handed me a single stamp, looking pleased with herself.

'I posted your letter.' She smiled.

I stared at the stamp and the penny dropped: she hadn't put the stamp on! I started to laugh, but Charlene had no idea why.

'Come here, you silly banana,' I laughed, pulling her in for a hug. The story went round the whole family and pretty soon Charlene herself was laughing when she realised how daft she'd been. Luckily, the letter was sent to some friends back in Coventry so they paid the postage when it arrived. It was one of those comical little reminders that make you realise your children are not quite as grown-up as you think. On Saturday mornings, we'd have half an hour on the couch and watch her Darren Day DVD, or an episode of *Supermarket Sweep* on video tape. It was Charlene's favourite programme. And afterwards, she'd insist on coming with me to the supermarket for our weekly shop.

'I'll push the trolley for you, Mummy.' She smiled.

Of course there was a catch. She'd tear up and down the aisles, recreating the TV programme, throwing in biscuits and cakes before I could stop her. I ended up spending twice as much as I'd intended every time she came. But I had to laugh. Like most girls her age, she was a walking contradiction of a badly behaved toddler and a maturing young woman. *And that was just it*, I reminded myself. *She was just the same as most girls her age.*

I resolved not to worry so much.

CHAPTER FOUR

MISSING

1st November 2003 started so unremarkably that I would later look back and wish I could have appreciated the normality, the nothingness; the humdrum boringness of it all. Because I would never, ever, know peace again.

It was a Saturday and so the house was less frantic. Charlene was up late in the morning, her hair tangled after her usual bath, swooning over her Darren Day DVD, as my mum served her egg on toast. She knew every single word of 'Summer Holiday'.

'Come on, eat up, Babby.' I smiled.

As I said earlier, it was my pet name for her and I still used it now, even though she was a teenager.

'I've lost one of my Reebok trainers,' she told me, in a break in the music. 'Have you seen it?'

I shook my head.

'The state of your room, could be anywhere,' I noted drily.

Charlene was still grumbling to herself about her missing trainer when I got ready to go shopping with my mum. Our neighbours had just had a new baby boy and so Charlene wanted to pop round and ask for a cuddle. Later, she and Becki were planning to meet up with their pals at the arcades.

'Here's your pocket money,' I said, handing her £5.

Becki had the same. By the time Mum and I got back from shopping, the girls were ready to go out. Charlene had a little denim bag, slung jauntily over her shoulder. I smiled secretly – I knew she thought it made her look grown-up.

'We might go to McDonald's for our tea,' Becki told me.

'Be good.' I smiled, half-distracted as I unpacked the frozen foods. Charlene was jaunty, bubbly. You could always tell she was giggling, even from the back. As the two girls walked off together, I saw her shoulders hunch a little and I knew she was having her usual laugh with Becki. There was no sense, none at all, of the all-consuming horror to come.

At 4:45pm, it was time for me to go to work, dropping leaflets for the local Indian restaurant. Mum came along to keep me company for the first hour, but it was filthy weather, drizzly and biting cold, and so I persuaded her to go home and warm up. It was the last weekend of the Illuminations, and it was busy with holidaymakers, despite the rain. As it was the day after Halloween, there were still plenty of over-enthusiastic children in horror masks and pointy witches' hats, trailing damp broomsticks and flickering wands behind them. I smiled and remembered back to when my own children were young enough to dress up. After Bob had been sacked from his job in Coventry, Trick or Treat night had lost its appeal because the area was so rough and I hated knocking on our neighbours' doors for fear of what reaction we'd get. But when we arrived in Blackpool, all that had changed.

It seemed the 'Blackpool effect' of turning each situation around had struck once again. Like a win on the penny arcades, every house was decked out with pumpkins and Halloween decorations. Each doorway was opened with a smile and a bag of sweets on offer. In the week before Halloween, Bob always used to help the kids make a guy, using old clothes stuffed with newspaper, and he gave them an old bobble hat. Charlene and Martin trundled around the streets, pushing the guy in an old dolls' pram, shouting: 'Penny for the Guy!' They made a fortune. One Halloween when the kids were young, Charlene dressed as a witch, Robert as a devil, and Bob took them round the streets, trailing a moulting broomstick and a plastic red pitchfork behind them. When they came home, pockets bulging with sweets and money, it was bonanza time in the living room.

'The place is like a sweet shop!' Mum gasped.

Charlene divided her spoils into equal piles for everyone. Even me and Bob got a share. And her nanna got the biggest share of all. She had a big heart for such a small girl.

'It's yours, darling.' I smiled, giving her back a handful of loose change. 'You keep it.'

They had been happy times. But kids grow up so fast and before I knew it, they had outgrown the Halloween costumes, the fake Dracula teeth and the face paints. And they turned their noses up when Bob wanted to carve out pumpkins and make a guy.

'Oh, Dad, not this year!' Charlene had told him, rolling her eyes as if it was all beneath her now.

Time had moved on, but that didn't stop me hankering back to those happy days. As I handed a leaflet to a couple with four children, all dressed as skeletons, I gave a fake scream of terror.

'My goodness!' I yelled. 'How scary!'

The children fell about laughing and scuttled off. It was nice to see. At 6:45pm, I spotted Charlene and Becki, drinking strawberry milkshakes and giggling yet again, as they walked down the street towards me. I could spot Charlene from miles away; she had on a pair of black jeans with gold dragons emblazoned on the front and a diamond patterned jumper. It was actually Becki's jumper and I could well imagine Charlene had helped herself without asking. She and Becki were close enough to clash and the sparks flew when they did. They would argue over clothes and shoes and drive me mad. Charlene liked to borrow Becki's jeans and tracksuits, but usually didn't ask first.

'Get out of my room!' Becki would screech. 'And take my clothes off!'

But tonight, Becki seemed to have softened – as older sisters often do – and had loaned her the jumper without a fight.

'Where's your coat, Charlene?' I admonished. 'It's cold.'

I knew she had forgotten to bring a coat on purpose because she was making the most of wearing the borrowed jumper – she wanted to show it off. But she laughed, just as she always did.

'Time you were getting home,' I told them.

Becki nodded. She was cold and shivering. But Charlene wanted to wait and meet one of her friends, Natalie, in the arcades.

'I've arranged to see her,' she told me. 'I can't let her down.'

'I'll wait as well,' I decided. 'Keep an eye on you.'

The air was thick with the smell of takeaways, and the gaudy shop lights blurred and bled into the gloom of the rain and mist. The Halloween costumes had carried themselves off home to bed. Only one lonely ghost, drifting past, was a reminder of the spooky season. Fifteen minutes later, Natalie's bus arrived, and Charlene kissed me and said: 'Love you, Mummy.'

Even at 14, she still called me 'Mummy' when nobody was listening. And I had to admit, I loved it.

'Don't be late home, darling,' I told her. 'I don't want you being late.'

I said it twice, for emphasis, hoping it would sink in. But Charlene seemed full of beans. Punctuality was low down on her list. Watching her walk away, happy, carefree, I smiled. Deep down, she was still my affectionate little girl. I felt, as mums sometimes do, a sudden and unexplained rush of love; the sort that makes your heart swell in your chest and you want to cry, partly because being a mum is the biggest privilege there is. And partly because it's such a fragile, hold-your-breath type of happiness that could be snatched away at any time. We were in the Las Vegas of the North, as Bob said – and even Las Vegas has its dark side.

* * *

It was 9:30pm by the time I arrived home from work. I had bought chips for everyone, Charlene included. My good mood had long since evaporated – my feet were killing me, I was soaked through, shivering and starving. All I wanted to do was get into my pyjamas, sit down and watch TV. But Bob met me at the door and rapped: 'Charlene isn't home yet, she's really pushing it this time.'

Inwardly, I groaned. This was the last thing I needed. But then, this wasn't exactly a surprise, it was absolutely typical of her lately. I was annoyed with her. I'd reminded her not to be late, I'd even repeated myself. But 10pm was her absolute cut-off time, so I knew she'd be in by then. I even put her supper out, ready.

'Well, if the chips go cold, that's her fault,' I said shortly.

But Bob was building himself up for a row, I could sense it.

'This has gone on long enough,' he said firmly. 'I won't have it. She's coming in and out as she pleases, she takes no bloody notice of me. You need to back me up.'

'Oh, Bob!' I sighed, carrying the plates through to the table. 'Can we leave it, just for tonight? I'm shattered, I want some peace.'

We ate our chips in silence. I felt sure, any moment, Charlene would come hurtling through the back door, wiping the last traces of lipstick off her face, moaning that her chips were cold and soggy. I was ready to give her such a good talking-to. But 10pm came and Charlene wasn't home. It was 2003, and so we had just one family mobile phone, shared between us, and Bob had it, as he usually took it to work with him. So we had no way of contacting her at all. Screwing up the chip papers, ready for the outside bin, I felt the first pangs of real worry. *Where was she?* I wrapped her chips again and put them by the microwave, ready for warming when she turned up.

'Do you know where she might be?' I asked Becki.

But Becki hadn't seen her since leaving her with me, just over three hours earlier.

'I haven't a clue where she is, Mum.' Becki shrugged. 'She'll probably be with her mates, she'll turn up.'

I nodded anxiously. She went off to bed, along with Emma. Little Robert was on a sleepover at his pal's. I had a number for Charlene's friend, Natalie, and so I rang, hoping to hear Charlene in the background.

'We left Charlene at the Carousel, at the end of the pier, at 9:30pm,' she told me. 'We had to go home to babysit and Charlene didn't want to come with us. She told us she was going home.'

My heart plummeted as she spoke.

'I'll go to the pier,' Bob said, grabbing his coat. 'Don't worry, Karen, I'll bring her back.'

Although I told myself there was a logical explanation, I couldn't settle. I was back and forth from the window, scanning the street. Time went on. There was no sign of her. The latest Charlene had ever stayed out was 10:30pm and even then, she was only round the corner at a friend's house and she hadn't let us know. This was so unlike her. I oscillated between worry and anger. Was she missing, or just misbehaving? I resolved to give her such a talking-to when she eventually showed up. The back door opened and my heart leapt – but from the heavy footsteps I knew instantly it was Bob. And we could see, from the expression on each other's faces, that there was no news.

'She's probably staying over with a friend, she'll be fine,' he reassured me. 'You know how kids are. You know how she is at the moment as well.'

I knew he was probably right, but Bob's uncharacteristic softness only served to accentuate how serious this was becoming. I appreciated his kindness, but at the same time, I didn't want it. I wanted him to rant and rave and for Charlene to come slinking back with the dawn, bleary-eyed and hardly apologetic.

'I'm going back out,' Bob said heavily. 'I'll take my push bike. You call the police, just in case there's been an accident.'

My heart thumping in my mouth, I dialled 999. It seemed so dramatic, so official, yet I felt it was the right thing to do. If nothing else, when Charlene did show up, I could make her see what a fuss she'd caused and how selfish she'd been. I played out the scene, in my mind, to reassure myself, more than anything.

'The police!' I would screech. 'We actually rang the P-O-L-I-C-E! Do you understand how serious this is, young lady? Do you actually realise what trouble you've caused?'

Charlene would look at her shoes and mumble an apology. But before I knew it, she'd be giggling and answering back.

'This will not do,' I would tell her.

And thinking back to my parenting course, I decided I would ground her for a month. I would stop her pocket money.

Set boundaries, I reminded myself. *Be consistent*.

I would show her who was boss. Oh yes, I certainly would. Just as soon as she got home ...

But the operator had answered now and she wanted to know which service I required.

'Police,' I said, in a tiny voice. 'Please.'

There was another pause and a new voice spoke.

'My daughter's missing,' I said anxiously. 'She's only 14.'

'Give her till morning,' said the operator.

He'd had barely enough time to think over my statement. I was stunned. And furious.

'She wouldn't do this, she wouldn't stay out all night,' I insisted. 'She's a child. I think she's in some sort of trouble.'

But he wouldn't budge. There was nothing for it but to sit and wait. Alone again, with the minutes dragging, I worked myself up into a panic. Charlene had only her £5 pocket money with her. Where the hell was she?

All night long, I waited, wide awake in the living room. Bob came back; he took the chair, I had the sofa. Neither of us even closed our eyes. The time dragged. Each second weighed heavier and heavier on my heart. A creak from the kids' beds upstairs, or the sound of the early milk-float in the street, sent me dashing for the door, thinking she was home. Her chips, now cold and congealed, sat sullen and lonely by the microwave. The first streaks of dawn shone into the house and Mum appeared in her pink dressing gown, her face etched with worry.

'Where could she be?' she asked.

I trudged upstairs to check the bedroom, but it was all exactly as Charlene had left it: her Darren Day posters smiling glibly from the walls, her hairbrush – a makeshift microphone – on the table. All so childlike, so innocent. Nothing was missing. I had to consider the possibility she might have run away, but there was absolutely no reason for her to do so. Yes, she was a handful, a little madam at times, but she was happy and loved. She was really looking forward to that coming Monday, too, when she was due to start at the Education Centre with Becki. She'd been on countdown, she was so excited – she'd got her own way, at last. Becki made the Centre sound like a day out and that, together with the idea of going somewhere with the big sister she idolised, was a big draw for Charlene. No, I couldn't see her running away, but I had to check, just to be sure.

My heart heavy, I called the police again.

'Give her 24 hours,' they said.

'She's been missing since last night. All night! She's 14,' I pleaded. 'She's a child.'

I felt like I was reporting a missing dog, not a young girl – they didn't seem to see the urgency.

Robert arrived home from his friend's. Emma and Becki surfaced, wanting breakfast. I panicked; wondering wildly what elaborate cover story I could tell them instead of the awful truth.

'Charlene still isn't home yet,' I said heavily.

Somehow, saying it out loud made it even worse. 'Yet' – such a small word, such significance. At times, during the night, I'd almost convinced myself there was a reasonable explanation, but seeing the fear and confusion on my children's faces, it was all suddenly and sickeningly real. I ushered Robert out of the way, and flicked the TV on for him. I wanted to shield him. The girls had no ideas, no suggestions of where she might be. I pleaded with them if there was anything they knew about Charlene – any secrets – to tell me.

'It's so important,' I stressed, the hysteria rising in my voice, despite myself.

But there was nothing. The girls insisted they were as stumped as I was. They had numbers for a few more of Charlene's pals and Bob called them all, but they didn't even realise she was missing. As far as any of us knew, Charlene didn't have a boyfriend, except little Martin, and they were just pals. I didn't for a moment think there was anything serious or sexual between them. All teenagers kept secrets from their parents, I wasn't daft enough to believe that Charlene was any different. But she just wasn't the sort to get involved in drinking or drugs or anything untoward. Though she liked to wear make-up and dress up and rebel, much of that was simply copycat behaviour, with having two older sisters. Deep down, she was very much a little girl, probably younger even than her 14 years. And that just worried me even more.

That day was agony. I didn't know what to do – I wanted to keep busy, but it didn't feel right, doing mundane jobs, with Charlene missing. I didn't want to wash the breakfast dishes, not until she was home. And I didn't want to put a wash on. I couldn't hoover. I couldn't throw away her chips. I couldn't carry on, like some demented housewife, knowing my baby was out there.

'Where is she?' Mum asked again, wringing her hands. 'If she'd stayed out with a friend, she'd be home by now. She'd be back for breakfast, you know she loves her food.'

Mum was right. As the minutes ticked by, my heart grew heavier.

'I think somebody has taken her,' I blurted out suddenly.

Bob and Mum stared, horrified. I wasn't even sure where the words had come from myself, but deep down, instinctively, that was what I felt: that my daughter had been kidnapped and was being held against her will.

'Don't talk bloody silly!' Bob said gruffly. 'I'll make you a brew. You're short of sleep, love, that's what it is.'

He brushed his arm across my back and again, the kindness killed me. I had a knot in my stomach as big as a football, threatening to choke me. Later in the morning, agitated and impatient, I went off on a trawl of Charlene's friends' houses. Then I called Martin.

'I didn't see her last night at all,' he told me. 'I don't know where she is. No idea.'

I went to see Natalie and her mum too. But they had no more information, nothing new from the night before.

'Isn't she back yet?' Natalie gasped.

I could see, just from her wide eyes, that she was genuinely shocked. I shook my head and wiped away tears.

'If she calls me, I will let you know straightaway,' Natalie promised. 'I'll ring everyone I know, I'll do my best.'

I nodded, too numb for gratitude. As I trudged home, I stared at every teenager in the distance, wondering if it was her. I peered into passing cars. I knew I must have looked like an oddball, but I didn't care.

When I got home, Bob had already gone out looking. Mum was cooking some lunch for the kids.

'I couldn't eat a thing,' I said quietly.

Martin called round and he was crying.

'I'm going out searching,' he told me. 'I'll find her for you.'

'Bless you.' I smiled. 'You're a good boy, Martin.'

That night seemed even longer than the one before. I stayed in the living room. Sometimes, in the darkness, my head drooped through sheer exhaustion and I dozed for a few moments. But snapping back awake, afterwards, I was flooded with the sickening realisation that Charlene was actually missing. That my daughter was out there – alone, vulnerable, scared. It was a nightmare no mother should have to endure.

CHAPTER FIVE

A SILENT NIGHT

It was Monday morning before the police finally came. Under protest, I packed Robert and Becki off to school and the Centre, and Emma off to work. I wanted to keep life normal for them, as much as I could.

'Will you ring us if she turns up?' Emma asked.

'Of course,' I promised.

Two uniformed officers arrived and took down Charlene's date of birth, her height, her weight. They wanted to know where she'd been, where she was going. It was all very routine for them. Not for me. They were kind, professional, but I felt swamped, helpless, as though I was drowning. This wasn't a role I wanted to play. I gave them two recent photos – one with Charlene smiling broadly, another was a school picture.

'It is likely she has run away,' said one officer.

His words were probably intended to reassure me, but instead I felt my cheeks flushing. They weren't taking this seriously at all.

'Absolutely not,' I insisted. 'She has never run away, she just wouldn't.'

I felt comforted that at least they were going to look for her. But I felt – no, I *knew*, for certain – that Charlene was not a runaway. And yet, where was she?

'Are you going to do a TV appeal?' I asked. 'I'll take part. I'm happy to do whatever it takes.'

But the officer shook his head.

'Not at this stage,' he said. 'I'm sorry.'

They left and I felt completely deflated – abandoned. Surely Charlene's photo should be on the front page of every newspaper, on every TV channel? These hours were crucial. We were losing valuable time.

'I think someone has taken her,' I said again to Bob. 'I can feel it.'

It was like a dark dread, creeping over me. A shadowy coat of fear no mother wants to wear. Bob put his arms out to me; he was suffering too. Yet we were alone in our trauma.

The kids came home.

'Isn't she back?' Becki asked, her voice shrill with anxiety.

'No,' I said feebly.

I hated to see them so worried. The hours dragged. That night was worse, if possible, than the one before. Because with each passing hour, it became less and less likely that my daughter was coming home. The next day, I saw officers doing house-to-house calls, with Charlene's photo. I expected some news; I thought they would call. But there was nothing. That night, again the silence, the emptiness, was stifling.

Where are you? I pleaded. But my voice was thin and pathetic in the darkness and no reply came. And with the worry and panic was a growing anger that nothing seemed to be happening.

'What are the police doing?' I complained. 'Why aren't they out searching?'

I felt like I was drowning – head bobbing, clinging on by my fingertips. And part of me wanted to let go and let the water take me. Because this pain was unbearable.

CHAPTER SIX
THE SEARCH

The following day, I got a call from the police to say they would send forensic officers to search the house.

'We need every little clue we can find,' explained our liaison officer, Julie Vigo. 'We might come across something which leads us to Charlene.'

I was pleased; that felt like a step forward. I didn't know what the search was for, but that didn't matter – I just wanted as much effort, as much activity, as possible. But when the van pulled up outside and 12 officers streamed into the house, wearing paper suits and shoes, I was alarmed. There was even a sniffer dog. I felt like I was under suspicion. They began turning the furniture upside down, emptying drawers, even examining the contents of the fridge.

'Drugs?' asked one accusingly, holding a syringe in the air.

'I'm diabetic,' Mum explained timidly. 'They're my syringes in the fridge.'

Then they came across a loose floorboard in the hallway.

'What happened here?' they asked. 'What have you got under here?'

I was confused; I had no idea why the board might be loose. The house was rented and the landlord had been doing some renovations. And I didn't really see the relevance. What did it matter?

'You could ask the landlord,' I said impatiently. 'That's nothing to do with us.'

I showed them Charlene's room. A small, crazy part of me almost thought we might find her hiding under the bed, in some sort of crazy prank. As a toddler, she had been through a phase of hiding every time I called her name. She would scurry behind a curtain with a muffled giggle, her shoes poking out underneath.

'Come on, Charlene,' I pleaded silently. 'Come out now. This has gone far enough, darling.'

But her room was cold, still and empty. There were no clues, no leads, not a shred. I hated to see her room disturbed. Mum and I went to sit with a neighbour until the search was finished. I managed to farm the other kids out with friends. Going back into the house at 8pm was harrowing, horrible. There were drawers emptied out in the bedrooms. The mattresses were standing on end, the carpets had been ripped up. It looked as though we'd been burgled, our lives were strewn out across the floor. I didn't know what they were looking for, or even if they had found it, but I imagined this was what happened when a child went missing. Truth was, I had no idea. Slowly, wearily, I began tidying, putting the remains of our home back together again.

'Leave it until tomorrow,' Bob said.

But the kids needed to go to bed. I had to start somewhere. Even little Robert's clothes were left in a big pile in his bedroom. His Liverpool FC quilt had been turned inside out.

'What's happened to my bedroom?' he wailed. 'And where's Charlene?'

It was a question none of us could answer. As I wrapped my arms around him, I felt his little body shudder as he began to sob. At 12 years old, this was too much for him to bear. Eventually, the kids settled down to bed and I stumbled into Charlene's room, weighed down with exhaustion and worry. I noticed, with a pang, that the forensic officers had taken her hairbrush and toothbrush. I knew they were just doing their job, but I felt as though I was losing her, piece by piece. I remembered her singing and dancing with that hairbrush, belting out Westlife and Darren Day. And there was the time she had learnt 'Silent Night' in German and she'd sung it in front of the mirror every night, swaying respectfully.

'*Stille Nacht, Heilige Nacht*,' she sang.

They were happy memories. Charlene was so much like me. As a little girl, I'd loved dancing. At primary school I'd been overweight, which sparked a long period of bullying and unhappiness. By the time I hit my teenage years, I was determined to turn things around. So, when a neighbour mentioned that her granddaughter was going for dance lessons, I was hooked – it sounded so glamorous and I was sure it was the perfect way to get thinner. I began pestering Mum and, though she didn't have much money, she could see how much it meant to me.

'Go on then,' she relented. 'Let's go down and see what it's all about.'

The following week I was enrolled at the Sylvia Bird Dance Centre. I was a bundle of nerves; a foolish mix of teenage giggles, sulks and blushes. But from the moment the music began, I loved it – I felt right at home. Before long, I was taking classes in ballet, tap and modern dance. Mum scrimped and saved and bought me a red blouse, a grey leotard and red tap and ballet shoes.

'I love them!' I squealed.

Every December, we put on a show. Like Charlene, I adored being onstage; I loved performing. I entered contests too, and won a gold medal for modern dance, a silver for tap and a bronze for ballet. And of course, as the years passed, the extra pounds I was carrying simply melted away.

You thought you were the bee's knees, Karen, I said softly to myself.

I even allowed myself a little chuckle. Not long afterwards, of course, I'd met Bob and his own dancing had blown me away – he could rock and roll like a pro. I watched, mesmerised, as he cartwheeled and flipped across the dancefloor: he was a gymnast, a dancer, a performer, all rolled into one. And so, our kids seemed destined to dance. Emma, like me, took lessons and she loved dancing in the clubs and bars of Blackpool. And Charlene, though she wasn't interested in dance school, was perhaps the best little mover in the family. I glanced at the CD player on her chest of drawers, where she would play her music full-blast.

'Turn it down!' Bob would shout, his voice booming up the stairs.

Little did he know I was in there with her, dancing and twerking to whatever silly music the kids were into. The two of us would giggle uncontrollably as Bob bawled: 'What are you doing up there? The ceiling is shaking, the light fittings are coming loose!'

Every year, on Mum's birthday, we'd see a show on the pier. One year, we saw the comedian Billy Pearce, the next, The Grumbleweeds band. Charlene loved the theatre, she was desperate to be onstage herself. After each show, we went backstage and met the stars.

'I'm going to be on the stage,' she told me seriously. 'I'm going to sing and dance and write letters to all my fans.'

Bob and I had even been to the Carousel bar with her. She and her friends would dance in there at the weekends. Mum came along too occasionally and Charlene's friends would cheer when she got up to do the actions to the 'Fast Food Song'.

'We wish we had a gran like Charlene's,' her friends said.

We didn't mind having a dance and a laugh with the kids; in fact, we loved it. That was the thing: I had thought I was close to Charlene, imagined I was on her wavelength. I made sure I knew her friends, I thought I knew where she was and who she was with. I wasn't one of those parents who had no idea what their kids were up to – or at least I thought I wasn't.

So, where was she now? I imagined her on the North Pier, lonely and alone, dancing in the dark. A tear rolled down my cheek. *Would I ever see her dance again?* I struggled to stem the rising panic whirling around the inside of my head. That night, I lay in her bed, grateful for any chance to feel close to her, greedily drinking in the smell from her pillow. I whispered the Lord's prayer quietly, fervently. And then, I found myself singing: 'Wheels On The Bus' and 'Baa Baa Black Sheep'. As a little girl, Charlene had loved those songs. But with each verse, my voice faded. I dozed a little, overcome by exhaustion, but I felt worse for it.

* * *

The next day was agony. Looking out of the window, I could see the street where Charlene and Martin had once skipped off happily to Sunday School. There were people passing right now, going about their daily lives as if nothing was wrong. How could the world just keep turning? It seemed so insensitive. So wrong.

'Where's my daughter?' I wanted to scream. 'Where is she?'

But my pleas were silent, my fear was my own. I felt like I was going down without a fight. Rigid with fear, I didn't move from the house in case she called, in case she came back. I sat by the window and fretted. That evening, just after I'd tucked Robert into bed, there was a knock at the door. A woman of about 40 stood on my doorstep; I had never seen her before.

'I've got some news about your daughter,' she said.

She seemed almost excited.

'Charlene?' I gasped. 'What? What is it?'

'I've seen her, sleeping in the bus station under a blanket,' she replied.

It took me a couple of minutes to take in her words, and before I knew it I was grabbing my coat and my bag.

'Come on, Bob!' I yelled.

A jumbled 'thank you' tumbled out of my mouth as we ran past the woman and off towards the bus station. It was only a couple of minutes away and we sprinted, our breath rasping, hearts pumping, all the way. Bob got there first, I followed close behind him.

'Where is she?' I asked. 'Can you see her?'

We split up and searched. There were commuters hurrying, there were day trippers wandering, carefree, with children in tow. But there was nobody sleeping under a blanket. Nobody at all. Broken, I crumpled into a heap on the pavement.

'She's not here, is she?' I sobbed.

Somehow, that little scrap of false hope was more deadly than all the worry and the stress of the previous week. I felt exhausted, crushed.

'That woman was a crank, love,' Bob said. 'After all, why would Charlene be sleeping here when she has a warm bed at home? It wouldn't even make sense.'

He was right. But for a few minutes, that slight sense of possibility had offered us a lifeline. And when it was cruelly snapped, we were left dangling, lower and darker than even before.

CHAPTER SEVEN
WHO IS MARTINA?

The day after, two officers came to the house and asked me, Bob and my mum to go to the station in turn. It seemed like progress. I thought maybe they had a lead, but Bob didn't think so.

'What do you want to talk to me for?' he growled. 'That won't help.'

'They need to do their job,' I cajoled him. 'Just co-operate, Bob. Please. It's all for Charlene.'

The last thing I needed was Bob losing his temper and putting his foot down.

'Leave him to me.' Mum nodded. 'You get your coat, Karen.'

The journey to the station seemed surreal. I had never been interviewed by the police before; I couldn't remember even being inside a police station. But I was happy to do anything – anything at all – if it meant bringing my daughter home.

The first officer seemed kind and sympathetic.

'This must be dreadful for you, Karen,' she said. 'So dreadful.'

But the second one fixed me with a glare as we sat down.

'Come on, Karen,' he said impatiently. 'You know where she is, don't you?'

I stiffened. It had never even occurred to me that they might think I was somehow involved.

'Is that a joke?' I stuttered. 'If I knew where she was, I would bring her straight home. You should be out there looking for her, not accusing me. I'm her mother, for goodness' sake!'

I understood that I had to be interviewed, but I hadn't expected this at all. The 'good cop, bad cop' routine was doubtless a strategy that worked for them. I calmed myself down, and revolting though the suggestion was, I didn't even mind being under suspicion as long as it helped them in the search for Charlene.

'I have no idea where she is,' I stated firmly. 'None at all.'

I explained, in painstaking detail, about the last time I had seen her, at 6:45pm on November 1, as I delivered leaflets in the drizzle – with no idea of how my life was about to fall apart.

'She wouldn't just vanish like this,' I said.

'Bob knows where she is,' said the second officer. 'But then, Bob has lots of secrets, hasn't he?'

I threw my arms out in frustration.

'What are you talking about?' I pleaded. 'We need help, not this!'

The officer levelled his gaze and said to me: 'Do you know who Martina is?'

The name meant nothing to me.

I said: 'Charlene has no friends called Martina, not that I know of.'

'Oh no,' he said dismissively, as if I was on the wrong track completely, 'you would need to ask Bob about Martina.'

The words oozed like slime from his lips. If he was looking for a reaction, I made sure he got none. And if Bob was having an affair with this woman, I really didn't care, not at that point. This seemed like trivial nonsense compared to the living hell we were facing.

'I haven't got time for this!' I snapped, though my heart was pounding. 'I don't want to talk about Bob or Martina, I want to get home in case there's any news from my daughter.'

But the questions weren't yet finished. Was there any reason for Charlene to leave home? Was she a happy girl? A troubled girl? What about her behaviour at school – her problems with discipline?

'I do struggle sometimes,' I admitted, blushing despite myself. 'But isn't that normal with teenagers? I do my best.'

'Maybe she ran away because she was unhappy at home,' they suggested.

'She hasn't run away,' I repeated, over and over, the tears streaming down my cheeks. 'I just don't know.'

And it was clear that the police didn't know either. One minute Bob and I were prime suspects. The next, they were saying Charlene was a runaway. They had no idea – and that frightened me even more.

Before leaving, I had to give a DNA sample. They took strands of my hair. Swabs from my mouth. Finger-prints. I felt violated and humiliated. I was shaking as I walked out, through the swing doors, into the grey winter drizzle.

'We're just doing our job,' explained the female officer. 'We have to rule you out.'

On the drive home, I realised they were right: it *was* part of the process, I just had to stay strong and calm. And I would do whatever it took to bring Charlene home. But as I got through my own front door, my mask slipped and I burst into tears.

'Have a brew, love,' Mum said, flicking on the kettle. 'They have no right to speak to you like that.'

Next, it was her turn to be questioned. Shell-shocked from my own grilling, I was worried how Mum would cope, at her age. She was 68 years old; she might have a heart attack or a stroke with all the stress.

'She's an elderly lady,' I told the officers. 'Please be gentle.'

I couldn't settle at all whilst she was out, but it was only just over an hour before I saw a car in the street and an officer helped Mum to the door.

'How was it?' I demanded.

She shrugged.

'I just told them what happened last Saturday,' she said. 'I told them the truth, as you did. What else can we do?'

Now it was Bob's turn to go in for an interview. He was indignant, leaving the house.

'You should be out there looking for her,' he told the CID officer furiously, 'not hassling me.'

I was worried about him losing his temper and making things worse – as if they could be any worse.

The hours passed and I tried to keep busy. But with the kids out, and Mum taking a nap, the house was quiet and I felt unsettled and jumpy. Charlene dominated my thoughts, but one minute, in the background of my mind, the name Martina popped up: who was she and how did she know Bob? Whilst he was out, I searched our bedroom. I wasn't even sure what I was looking for. As I rummaged under his clothes, I suddenly came across a neatly rolled bundle and I knew instantly, from the cheap, scratchy lace, exactly what it was. My breath caught in my throat and a wave of sickness sloshed over me. Slowly, I unrolled a burgundy coloured pair of knickers, a black bra and a pair of tights. Hidden inside a T-shirt was a bottle of red nail polish. I didn't wear nail polish myself, none of this belonged to me. Already at breaking point, I was struggling to take this in. There were a million possibilities, all equally outlandish. The only way forward was to speak to Bob myself. Then the door banged, the children came home and I forced a smile.

'Where's Dad?' they asked.

'He's helping the police,' I said uncertainly. 'It's what happens when a child goes missing. Apparently.'

I called the police station, but was told Bob was still being interviewed. Like a robot, I cooked tea and washed the dishes. A few days earlier I hadn't been able to face this, but now I knew I had to carry on. As banal as it sounded, my children wanted to eat and play and argue, yet I felt like a mad housewife in the most macabre of comedies. My youngest daughter was missing and my husband had ladies' clothes stashed in his bedside cabinet, but I was happily serving up oven chips and fish fingers like it was all part of normal life. I had such tension, such fury, bubbling inside me that I felt like smashing the metal cooking tray over my own head. But then the sound of my three children, bickering over the spare fish finger, jolted me back to my senses – I had to be strong for them.

You're a mother, Karen, I reminded myself.

Yet I was a mother with a child missing. Her voice whirred around inside my head. I thought about our last meeting, where she had giggled despite the cold and sauntered off with her friend. *Where was she now? Where was she?* I tormented myself to the point of madness.

It grew dark, and there was no word from Bob. I took up my station, by the window, looking out for Charlene. Finally, a whole 16 hours later, the door slammed and Bob marched in. He was grey and shaking with rage.

'They think it's me,' he announced bitterly. 'They think I took Charlene. They asked me if I killed her, my own daughter.'

There was a silence, where the weight of his words hung heavily on us both.

'They're just doing their job,' I said, measuring my words carefully. 'Let's stay calm.'

But Bob was like a broken man. He looked shorter, smaller than usual. *Perhaps he hadn't been eating properly*, I thought, *since Charlene had gone. Or maybe this whole nightmare was dragging him down physically.* The small piece of my heart that wasn't already ripped to pieces went out to him yet I couldn't bring myself to give him a hug or to comfort him, I just didn't have it in me. And normally, of the two of us, I was the more tactile one – I always like a cuddle. But I wasn't even sure who this man was. He sat down next to me on the sofa and, mentally and physically, I edged away.

'They asked me where the body is,' Bob spat. 'Can you believe that? The cheek of them!'

'Can't you see it's just part of their routine?' I said wearily. 'They really don't think it's you, Bob. Calm down.'

But he was blazing.

'They accused me of pimping her out, selling her to other men for sex,' he choked. 'Good God, Karen! What next?'

I was horrified. We were supposed to be the victims, the two people in the world who loved Charlene the most, yet we were being treated without a shred of respect or consideration. I had no idea if this was how investigations were supposed to work – I knew nobody in our situation, our nightmare. Things like this just didn't happen to people like me. Worse still, this wasn't helping to bring Charlene home. If they thought it was Bob, then they weren't out there, looking for the real suspects.

Bob banged out of the room and I supposed he was off to bed. But I was far from sleep. In the quiet of the living room, I sat by the window, in the shadows, gazing out onto an empty street, rigid with fear, sagging with exhaustion. My heart ached for a glimpse of Charlene.

Bob came back downstairs and I could hear him fidgeting uncomfortably behind me. Realising why he was there, and sensing his agony, I summoned the last dregs of my emotional strength.

'Who is she?' I asked quietly, turning to face him. 'Who's Martina?'

His face contorted into a cathartic mixture of pain, shame and relief.

'It's me, Karen. *I'm* Martina.'

I stared, bewildered.

'When the forensics searched the house, they found counselling records for a woman called Martina Peters,' he continued.

Through the gloom of the darkened room, I realised he was shaking. His eyes were glistening with tears. He explained, in almost a whisper, that he'd been having secret counselling, for transgender tendencies, for two years. But he'd had feelings about becoming a woman for a long time before that.

'I saw a doctor, but I wasn't sure I could go the whole way, into becoming a woman,' he explained nervously. 'It's what I want – at least, I think it is. But I couldn't put you and the kids through that, so I've been seeing a counsellor to try to sort through my feelings.'

'Two years!' I gasped, my voice rising despite myself. 'How come I didn't know?'

Was I the most stupid woman in the world? My daughter had vanished and for two years I hadn't noticed my husband was transgender. And I hadn't a clue what was going on. I wondered, irrationally maybe, whether it was my fault. *Had I driven him to it, in some way? Should I have spotted the signs?*

'Don't you fancy me?' I asked in a small voice. 'Are you gay? What is it?'

Bob shook his head.

'I've never been attracted to men,' he said. 'That's not how it is. I love you, Karen – I always will.'

The underwear I'd found belonged to him, he said, and he wore it when me and the kids were out. He even put on the nail varnish.

'You dress up, whilst we're out?' I repeated.

I couldn't believe it. He had kept it all secret, all nicely wrapped up and separate, until the police turned our house upside down.

'The police think I might have killed Charlene because she caught me dressing up as a woman,' Bob choked. 'That's their theory. But it's just not true. Nobody knew … Nobody except my counsellor.'

I realised this was a horrendous predicament for Bob, but I didn't know how to comfort him. I was totally dumbfounded. Bob was a man's man. He had worked as a doorman and a security guard. He enjoyed a pint every Sunday lunchtime, he had lots of male friends and he was a strong father figure. Sure, he'd change nappies and play with the kids, but he did the discipline too; his heavy-handedness was what had caused so much trouble between us. He was, without question, the man of our house. This was the last thing I could ever have imagined. It was fair to say we'd had our ups and downs: we disagreed over the kids, I didn't like his short fuse. His temper had even driven me into the arms of another man, years before. But weren't all marriages like that? You picked yourself up, you made the best of what you had and you soldiered on. There'd been long periods without sex too, but that was hardly unusual for a middle-aged couple with four kids. We'd thought that moving to Blackpool might help, but I'd had no idea, none at all.

I wondered whether his rages might perhaps have been a symptom of the frustration and repression he was feeling. I'd always presumed his temper was a sign of his masculinity. Perhaps it was quite the opposite. Did he hide behind his temper? Because of his outbursts – or perhaps despite them – I hadn't suspected. I just didn't know. It was a bombshell alright. And yet, with our daughter missing, it wasn't quite the cataclysmic shock it might have been. There were many things I didn't know about my husband, but one thing was sure, he was no killer. And like me, he was torn in two about his missing girl.

'I'm sorry,' he whimpered, and I felt my heart break for what seemed like the thousandth time.

I felt a rush of sympathy for him. There was no anger, just shock and a deep sense of sadness for him. He had carried this all alone, for so long.

'But why didn't you tell me?' I asked. 'Why live a lie for so long?'

'I thought you'd leave me,' he said. 'I still want you to be my wife, I want a family. I can't explain Martina, I really can't.'

'I'll support you,' I said limply. 'I won't leave you, Bob.'

If he didn't understand it, then I had no chance – I had no experience of transgender issues. But what I couldn't believe was that we'd lived together for so long and I hadn't once suspected a thing. I had fallen for Bob, all those years earlier, because he had seemed so solid and reliable. The idea seemed quite ridiculous now. I'd felt certain he would never let me down. And of course, he still hadn't. I had to remember that. In fact, he'd gone to great lengths to make sure his feelings hadn't affected our family life. I was grateful for that and I admired him for it – hugely.

My mind went back to the night we'd first met, as teenagers, in a dance hall in Coventry. Bob had caught my eye in his white satin shirt. I remembered thinking the shirt would suit me too. *Had that been a clue?* He loved Elvis; he was slimmer back then, and he jived all over the dance-floor, in his shiny shirt, like he owned the place. He had always loved dancing and he would swing his hips and sway – and yes, maybe more like a woman than a man.

'Are you sure he's not gay?' my dad had asked, the first time he saw Bob dance.

But it was said as a joke, a throwaway line. And Dad was from a generation where men didn't dance, so I paid no attention to it. I had always loved Bob's dancing, but was that the start of it – the birthplace of Martina – whoever she was? And after we moved in together, I'd found it comical that Bob had two baths a day. He insisted on it. He'd have one bath before work and one afterwards. He was fanatical about hygiene; he had more deodorants and smellies than me and Mum put together.

'Bob, you spend more time in that bathroom than any woman I know!' Mum teased. 'You'll have to have your own vanity cupboard for all that stuff you wear.'

But his efforts paid off, because Bob always smelled lovely. He took such great pride in his appearance and his personal care. Was that the woman inside him – struggling to come out – or struggling to stay in? And though Bob had a rough exterior, he had a vulnerability, the fragility of a little boy lost, which pulled at my heartstrings. I had always had the sense that he needed looking after, that sometimes what he needed was a mother rather than a wife. But how many other wives had I heard moaning about the very same thing?

I had one pal who joked she had brought her husband up, along with their children. Bob was emotionally immature, stunted even. But so many men were exactly the same. He'd always been unusually soft and gentle too with any animals we had. He'd had an Alsatian dog called Rebel for years, followed by a cat named Blackie. He adored them both and had been bereft when they died. But just because he loved animals, I could hardly have foreseen that he might want to wear my clothes. It was something of a seismic leap. Bizarrely, I found myself stifling a giggle, the sort of uncontrollable laughter that grips you in church or in a school exam hall. Then, with a jolt, I realised that was exactly the sort of thing Charlene always did; she giggled her way through everything, however inappropriate. And suddenly the laughter died in my throat and mutated into a strangled sob. Bob took me in his arms and for a few minutes, we cried together. There were endless questions, for our family, our marriage, our future. But the way I saw it, there was no future, no family, until Charlene came home.

'Come to bed, Karen,' he said. 'It's late, we've had a hell of a day.'

The understatement of the year. But going to bed was no longer an option for me – I couldn't rest or relax.

'I'm sorry,' I said.

Bob's eyes were filled with rejection, his shoulders sagged.

Jessie Hall, my grandmother, holding Charlene (aged three months) at her christening in Coventry.

Left to right: Emma (5), Becki (3), Charlene (18 months).

Charlene, aged 7, with her cousin Katie Brown in the garden.

Charlene in her new high school uniform, aged 11, with a short haircut she didn't like!

Charlene, aged 13, with her long hair back. Here she is waiting to see Darren Day at Blackpool's Winter Gardens.

Charlene lying on the couch, aged 13, shortly before her disappearance, pictured in our Blackpool home.

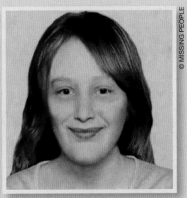

Charlene's bus pass photo, aged 13, February 2003 – the year she disappeared.

An image, created by university researchers, of how Charlene might look now.

Flowers at Charlene's memorial bench.

My mum Jessie (left) and me (right) on her birthday.

Me with newborn Tallulah, my granddaughter.

I went to lie on Charlene's bed, just to close my eyes and feel near to her. Bob went to bed alone. I knew he felt pushed out on the very night when he needed me most. But Charlene needed me more.

I felt, if I reached out to her, in my mind, I might be able to touch her. I had carried her for nine months: her bones, her blood, her mind and soul had all been created in my womb. That surely gave us a connection which would, in times of great fear and trauma, transcend all boundaries? I felt certain I could find her if I was in her room, surrounded by her.

CHAPTER EIGHT
UNWELCOME ATTENTION

Word of Bob's police interview spread quickly through the local community. One of our neighbours called to see how he was. She was a woman I hardly knew; she had certainly never knocked on our door before.

'We wondered how Bob is feeling,' she said.

What she really meant was: 'Tell us all the gossip.'

'We're fine,' I said shortly, trying to bite back my anger. 'Really, we're fine.'

I didn't have it in me to be rude to her. But I was fast becoming cynical. It felt like we were turning into some sort of soap opera. The whole street was talking about us, or so it seemed. I took up my usual position, at the window, and was alarmed to see passers-by pointing and staring at our house, as if we were some sort of freak tourist attraction.

'They'll all calm down,' Mum assured me. 'As soon as Charlene comes home, life will get back to normal. She'll walk in through that door any minute, Karen. Mark my words.' But her voice quavered as she said it. We both knew she was lying to herself and to me.

That night, Bob grabbed his wallet and keys, as he usually did, and said: 'I'm off, then.'

I stared, amazed.

'Are you going to the pub tonight?' I asked. 'With everything that's going on?'

At this Bob rounded on me like I was the cause of his problems.

'I've as much right to a drink as anyone,' he rapped.

And he was gone.

Mum and I spent the evening waiting, watching, weeping.

'Where do you think she is?' I asked her. 'What's your gut feeling?'

Over the past few months, Mum had been closer to Charlene than any of us. And even before that, they had been good pals. Surely she might have a suggestion?

She sighed.

'I don't know where she is,' she said sadly. 'But I do know she wouldn't run away. I feel certain of that, and I told the police so too.'

She put her hand on mine and said the Lord's prayer out loud. I closed my eyes and wished and hoped like I'd never done before. And then suddenly, the back door slammed with such ferocity that the whole house seemed to shudder. We were snapped out of our meditation. Bob strode into the living room, swearing and steaming with anger.

'One bloke spat at me in the pub,' he seethed. 'Some idiot called me a murderer. Another bloke asked me why I was out drinking and why I wasn't looking for Charlene. Said I shouldn't be out drinking whilst she's missing. These people have no idea, none at all.'

I was shocked. These men were not strangers, they were men he had been drinking with for years; he counted some of them amongst his friends. I was amazed they had turned against him.

'Can't you just stay out of the pub for a while?' I pleaded. 'We have enough to cope with.'

Really, I was dumbfounded that he could even think of going out drinking. To me, it seemed that he was stoking up trouble, arguing with everyone. We had enough to cope with. But I knew that Bob had his own way of doing things and there was nothing I could do to change his mind.

The next night, after searching for Charlene all day, he was back in the pub. For a couple of nights, things seemed to calm down. But then he staggered home with his nose bleeding and his eyes purple and swelling.

'What the hell happened?' I gasped.

He had been attacked and beaten up – people thought he had killed his own daughter.

'Let's call the police,' I said. 'We can't have this.'

But he wouldn't hear of it.

'It won't bring Charlene back,' he said flatly. 'I don't want any fuss.'

I thought this would be the final straw and that he'd at least stay at home from now, but still, he didn't give up: he found another pub to drink in. I waited at home, on tenterhooks, wondering what fresh tale of horror he'd bring home that night. When the door slammed, I was on edge. I smelled him before I saw him; he stank of beer.

'Well?' I asked, eyeing his wet hair and shirt.

'Isn't it bloody obvious?' he growled. 'The barman took my money and instead of giving me my pint, he chucked it over my head. There were blokes shouting that I had pimped my own daughter out. I had to get out before they lynched me.'

He sunk onto a chair, head in his hands, like a beaten man. His daughter was missing, he needed help and support, and yet he was being ostracised. He had become an outcast in his own neighbourhood.

'This is the police, they've done this,' he said. 'They question me, they do bugger-all else. People put two and two together.'

'Don't worry, Bob,' I said quietly. 'Your family know you didn't do it. And that's what's important.'

I knew he was under a lot of stress. It wasn't fair or just or humane. Normally, I would have been outraged at what he was going through. And yet his pain, however undeserved, hardly registered with me. I was almost irritated by the distraction. All I could think of was Charlene. I knew we should be sticking together; holding each other, staying strong. But that sort of thing isn't so easy in real life. Instead, I shut myself off from him. I took his sodden clothes, clicked the washer on and then carried on straight upstairs to bed. I left him sitting in the living room, in his vest and undies, staring at the wall with silent tears streaming down his face. The best person to cling to when you're drowning, I realised, is not the one who is drowning with you. We needed a lifeboat and a rescue crew.

But there was nothing on the horizon, nothing at all. That week, I spent hour after hour in Charlene's room, rocking back and forth, clutching her teddies. I went over and over the details of her disappearance until I was weary and sick to death of myself and my thoughts. Meanwhile, Bob cycled round, searching, during the day. Time after time, he'd go back to the Carousel. He checked all the arcades. He spoke to the cashiers and the assistants. He grilled the cleaners and the security guards. There was nothing. No CCTV. No witnesses. At night, weary with despair, he'd find a pub where nobody knew him.

'For God's sake, Bob, just stay away from the pubs!' I snapped.

How much more could we take? Our wound was already gaping and he wanted to pull it open wider. And he didn't listen. At the start of the second week, his sister, Sharon, and her husband, Tony, called from Coventry and announced they were coming to join the search.

'She'll turn up, Karen,' Sharon assured me. 'We'll keep looking until we find her, I promise. A girl can't just vanish, she must be somewhere.'

They arrived with a family friend, Des. Tony drove around Blackpool, for hours at a time, searching.

'Have you considered she might have fallen into the sea?' he asked anxiously.

But I shook my head firmly. The thought had occurred briefly to me; after all, Charlene was last seen on the pier. But, like me, she was rather scared of water. Although she could swim, she didn't enjoy it. She certainly wouldn't have gone near the water for a dare or a bet.

'That wouldn't be like her,' I said. 'She wouldn't go in the sea, she never even walks to the end of the pier.'

Yet I was starting to wonder what exactly Charlene *was* like. Because although I knew where she wouldn't be, I had no idea where she would be. And as each day passed,

I began to doubt myself more and more. Every morning, little search parties would leave our house, in twos and threes. At the start of a new day, there was always hope, always possibility. At the end of it, they tramped back, damp with Blackpool drizzle, all hope crushed.

'We have to carry on,' I insisted stoically. 'We *have* to.'

But it was hard; it felt so futile. We needed something to pick us up, a morsel of good news. Then, at the end of the second week, the police called.

'We may have a sighting of Charlene,' said an officer.

My heart was in my mouth.

'Where?' I stuttered. 'When?'

Bob was already getting his coat on, in the background, ready to go and collect her. But the officer wouldn't give us any more information.

'It's not confirmed at this stage,' he said apologetically. 'We'll check it out as soon as we can. Please don't pin your hopes on this.'

But that was easy to say. I hung on to every word he said like it was chocolate oxygen. Was this it? Was she safe – at last? Giddy with optimism, I was waiting for more news, hovering over the phone. It was hours before the call came that sent me plummeting into despair, all over again.

'I'm sorry, it wasn't Charlene,' said the officer. 'We've tracked the girl down, it's not your daughter.'

I hung up and sobbed.

'The search goes on,' Bob said. 'We won't give up.'

* * *

At the end of November 2003, our family had to eventually return to Coventry; to their jobs, their lives, their normality. But for us, life had gone crazy. Total strangers began knocking on my door and throwing their arms around me. Friends brought flowers. In the supermarket, other mothers, who I barely knew, would burst into tears on my behalf.

'You're the mum of the missing girl!' they exclaimed.

It was odd, I noticed, how people who never normally gave me a second glance – who probably didn't even like me very much – were suddenly sobbing at my plight, like they were all hopping on the grief bus. It was a nasty, cynical thought and I was surprised at myself. But there it was. Through all of this I was discovering a side of me that I didn't like too much. I was grateful, of course, for any genuine sympathy, but I was angry too. Living in a permanent state of anticipation was wearying. And my patience – like my temper – was stretched thin like an overblown balloon.

'So sorry,' they simpered. '*So* sorry. We can't begin to imagine what you're going through.' That was their way of saying: 'So glad it's you, not me. What a relief it's your daughter, not mine.'

I was a mother trapped in everyone's worst nightmare. To the outside world, I was a victim: pitied, not judged, but not fully believed either. They'd bring me flowers, but they didn't bring their children round to play. Because nobody really knew; nobody really knew what had happened to Charlene. And I was not to be trusted. Not completely. As I threw another bunch of flowers onto the kitchen worksurface Bob snarled: 'That's fine! You get the sympathy, I get the beatings.'

I stared at him in disbelief, contempt bubbling in my throat.

'This is not about you or me,' I choked. 'This is about our daughter.'

CHAPTER NINE

FALSE HOPE

Those first weeks, there were lots of sightings. And though I told myself, school-teacher like, not to get carried away, it was impossible. I kept most of the reports, as much as I could, secret from the children, so they didn't get their hopes up. I kept them busy too, tried to stick to their usual routines, to help them cope. I insisted that the girls saw their friends, and that Robert played football, though I made sure they all stayed close to home. It helped take their minds off Charlene, if only for an hour here and there. But I was stuck riding an eternal emotional rollercoaster of ups and downs, of rising hope and crushing despair. I could not have felt more disorientated if I had been on the big rides on the Pleasure Beach on one long nauseating loop.

One afternoon, in early December 2003, a middle-aged woman knocked on my door and handed me the obligatory flowers. I had never seen her before but she seemed very agitated. Immediately, my heart quickened. I thought that maybe she had some good news for me.

'Mrs Downes?' she began. 'I'm sorry about Charlene, I just heard they found her body on the railway line.'

Clutching the doorframe as my legs buckled, I gasped for air. Bent double, I retched onto the pavement.

'Get away!' I screamed. 'You filthy liar!'

I threw the flowers after her, consumed by an anger that terrified me. Slamming the door, I called the police, my fingers too clumsy for the buttons.

'Charlene …' I stuttered. 'Have you found her? Is she dead?'

'There's no news,' the liaison officer told me. 'The woman is a crank, ignore her.'

Mum ran out into the street after her, waving her arms, shouting. But the woman had fled.

There were more sightings, more glimmers of hope. But now, I was trying hard to temper my expectations. My sudden immersion into the cold world of missing persons had taught me, in a short, sharp lesson, not to believe everything – or even anything – I was told. The world seemed to be full of oddballs. Someone else claimed they'd seen Charlene at the train station, boarding a train to Manchester. Again, I rang the police. But it was another hoax.

'We've checked all the CCTV,' they assured me.

Desperate to be sure, I went down to the station myself and asked at the ticket office.

'She's 14, long brown hair,' I explained, tears brimming.

'Sorry, love,' said the cashier.

Even so I searched the platforms, peered into the ladies' loos. I didn't quite know what I was doing, or what I was expecting to find, but I had to keep going.

The next week, there was another report. And another. I dashed from one landmark to another, searching for the holy grail. Yet every sighting – every crumb of expectation – turned out to be someone else's daughter.

'What about my Charlene?' I wept. 'Where is she?'

There was no sign of this rollercoaster stopping or even slowing and I felt sick with desperation. The manic laughter from the Pleasure Beach theme park and the bright lights of Blackpool took on a sinister, threatening air. As I searched, I started to notice the dark alleyways. The grubby take-aways. This was a town of false promise. I felt trapped and alone, in a dark tunnel, clawing my way through, with no end in sight. And I felt so guilty, especially at night; safe, in a nice, clean home. I slept in Charlene's room, curled up under her pink 'Groovy Chicks' quilt cover, sobbing myself into some sort of broken, tortuous sleep. Mum was in the bed next to me, her eyes heavy with pain. I'd catch her staring at me, her face creased with concern. I was an only child, she a single parent, and we shared the closest of bonds. When my own daughters were born, I had hoped we'd have the same relationship right through their lives.

'Can I make you a cup of tea?' Mum asked, as I stared into the darkness, in silence. 'Warm you up, Karen?'

I knew, as a mother, she just wanted to make me feel better. Over the years, tea had been a comfort for many things: teenage heartbreak, money troubles, squabbles with Bob. Even as a child, a cup of tea could always bring a smile to my face. In the last year at primary school, I'd been bullied because of my weight. A chubby child, I was shy and self-conscious too. One girl – the ringleader of the class – made my life a misery.

'Fatso!' she jeered. 'Honey Monster!'

Crimson with shame, I ran all the way home, tears dripping off the end of my nose. I was 11 years old and, as for all children of that age, it felt like the end of my very small world. Mum listened patiently whilst she brought me a hot cup of tea and a Rich Tea biscuit.

'I know the girl you mean!' she exclaimed. 'She has a nose like Captain Hook, Karen. I don't know what *she* has to brag about!'

We both dissolved into helpless laughter.

Then, that summer, my dad, Bill, came to visit and announced he had a new girlfriend, Margaret.

'Margaret says you can come for tea,' he told me. 'Fancy it?'

I was so excited. Dad had walked out when I was a baby and had never shown much interest in me, so him taking notice of me like this was wonderful. Mum wasn't too impressed, but she allowed me to go.

Dad's house, when we arrived, took my breath away – it was huge in comparison to mine and Mum's. There was a garden, front and back. And when I took off my shoes at the front door, my feet seemed to sink into the plush carpets.

'I love your house,' I told him.

But there was no sign of Margaret. Eventually, a voice called me upstairs and a woman with a sharp face glared at me and threw some papers at me.

'Your mother's a bitch!' she snarled. 'She's wicked. Read the divorce papers!'

Screaming, I ran down the stairs and begged to go home. When Mum saw the state I was in, she flew at Dad – I had never seen her so angry. But afterwards, she flicked on the kettle, got out the biscuits and smiled.

'We'll have a brew,' she said. 'And we'll forget that horrible woman ever existed.'

And again, when my babies came, Mum was there with the biscuits and the tea. Charlene would be awake for hours during the night – there was nothing I could do to settle her. But just as I was feeling alone and desperate, Mum would peer round the doorframe with a gummy smile, her teeth still in a glass by her bed.

'I'll make us a brew,' she whispered. 'Fancy a biscuit?'

And through my exhaustion, I beamed. It could be 2am or 4am, but Mum didn't seem to care. She'd sit up with me, rocking Charlene, as we took it in turns to sing 'Wheels On The Bus' and work our way through a packet of cure-all Rich Teas.

'You always feel better after a cuppa,' she insisted.

And she was right. What a remedy! Broken hearts, bruised egos, hurt feelings ... Mum's tea and biscuits always did the job.

Until now. Night after night, Mum lined up cups of tea on my bedside table. Untouched, each one gradually grew lukewarm and curdled. I didn't want tea and I didn't want comfort, I wanted to suffer like my Charlene. What if she was huddled up outside somewhere? What if she'd been kidnapped, held against her will? Or worse? When sleep overpowered me, it was only for a few minutes at a time. My sleep was infected with violent images of Charlene, bound, gagged, tortured.

'Mummy!' she shouted. 'Mummy, I'm here!'

Looking round wildly in the dream, I reached out desperately for her – but never found her. And then, I was awake. It hit me with a sickening jolt, all over again: a wave of panic, fear and guilt. How could I rest whilst my little girl was out there? Sinking into a pit of depression and despair, I felt a growing distance between me and Bob. He drank too much, I cried all the time – we both had different ways of coping. Of *not* coping. When I wasn't sitting by the window, watching the street, I'd be in Charlene's bedroom. From her bedroom, I was over-looking the street below and the car park where she and Martin had often played. Poor Martin; he was so fragile and whenever I saw him he would burst into tears.

'I'm doing all I can,' he promised me. 'I'm always out looking for her.'

He seemed lost without his best pal. We were all lost without Charlene. In some ways, being in her bedroom brought me closer to her. Straightening the bedcover, I could almost pretend she was coming home that night.

'Why don't you come back into our bed?' Bob asked awkwardly.

It had been five long weeks since he and I had shared a bed. But I shivered and shook my head.

'I couldn't,' I said, sounding harsher than I'd meant. 'Whilst Charlene is missing, I need to be there, in her room.'

I couldn't bear to be near him. But it wasn't because of Martina, as he thought, though God knows, that had rocked me to the core. My main thought, my *only* thought – my reason for breathing, for battling on through this hell – was Charlene. I didn't want comfort or warmth or pleasure, not whilst my baby was out there suffering. It just didn't seem right. But did I sleep in Charlene's bed to be close to her, or was I avoiding my husband? My thoughts were so tangled, I hardly knew. Shameful to think I might be using my daughter's disappearance to get out of sleeping with him, a low amongst lows. But I'd had so much shame and pain and agony heaped on my shoulders of late, I didn't much care what he thought any more.

'I'll be in Charlene's bed until she comes home,' I told him shortly. 'I just feel it's the right thing to do.'

Bob skulked off without another word but I could almost feel him radiating a humiliation so deep it would scar him forever.

* * *

I couldn't face returning to work, dropping leaflets. Besides, the whole point of my little job had been to earn a few extra pounds to cheer us all up. My wage bought takeaways or treats on a Saturday, or paid for the odd day out. That was futile now; all that mattered was bringing my daughter home. So I asked the police, if, instead, I could hand out leaflets about Charlene.

'Can't do any harm,' they said. 'It's a good idea.'

They even had leaflets printed for me, with her photo on, and a description of the clothes she was wearing.

The first night was surreal as I retraced my steps from that fateful evening, past the bus stop where I'd spent those last few minutes with Charlene, down towards the pier where she had inexplicably vanished. I remembered the children in their Halloween costumes. I'd laughed at the mock horror with no idea of the real-life terror that awaited me. I thought back to the little ghost, drifting along the pavement, long after all the others had gone home. Had that really happened? I no longer knew. Reality had become so unbearable that the borders were blurred. It was almost like a macabre magic trick, from one of the acts on the North Pier: The Vanishing Girl. If the dark forces had taken her, where was the White Witch who would bring her back? Night after night, I'd walk a well-trodden route through Blackpool, with my daughters, and my mum, pleading with people to take a leaflet.

'Have you seen her?' I asked. 'Please, take a good look. It's my daughter – and she's missing. And she's just a child.'

It was hard. Some people would laugh, others would swear – or, and this was hard to take – they would just ignore us. One woman hit us with an umbrella and shouted as though *we* were the ones behaving disrespectfully. It hadn't mattered so much when I was handing out leaflets for samosas and bhaajis, it was – quite literally – life and death. And it was harder still when someone took a leaflet and dropped it casually, yards down the road, into the gutter, without so much as a glance. Seeing Charlene's smiling face, staring up at me from a wet pavement, was soul-destroying. Of course there were kind souls too, who took my leaflets and promised to look out for Charlene. There were mothers who took me in their arms and one who wept with me when she heard my story.

'There but for the grace of God,' she said. 'It could happen to any of us, any mother.'

One night, in the crowd, I spotted a girl with wavy brown hair, her shoulders slightly hunched as though she was giggling. From the back, she looked the double of my daughter.

'Charlene!' I screamed. 'Charlene!'

Pushing my way through, I elbowed holidaymakers to get to her. And then, as she turned to face me, my heart sank.

'Sorry,' I mumbled. 'Wrong girl.'

It happened time and time again. I would be midway through handing out leaflets when I'd spot a girl wearing Charlene's jumper or her trainers. Convinced I had to see every face that went past, in case it was her, I drove myself mad. I found myself scurrying after people, pushing through the crowds, to get to her.

'Sorry,' I said, as I bundled into yet another startled teenage girl. 'I thought you were …'

I trailed off; I couldn't bring myself to say it. I'd run alongside the buses and the trams too, in case she was on there, breathless and gasping as they pulled away and picked up speed. I couldn't walk past a single alley or side street, because the one I missed, I told myself, would be the one where she was being held hostage. Sometimes, I would wander for hours, searching, stumbling, blind drunk on the pure pressure and emotion. And on those soul-splintering nights, in the dark and the drizzle, I saw a different side to the Kiss-Me-Quick fun of Blackpool we had once loved. There were groups of girls, scantily-dressed, half-frozen, far too young to be out on their own.

'Just like my Charlene,' I said sadly.

I spotted middle-aged men, lurking outside the arcades and the bars. There was an air of garish malevolence about the town now; the shops looked gaudy and grimy. I had brought my children here – right into the lions' den. I had followed my husband without question and look where it had got me: I was a mother who needed parenting classes. A mother with failings, shortcomings, inadequacies. And now, I was a mother without a child. I blamed myself for it, and how I hated myself.

'Las Vegas of the North,' Bob had told us.

'All that glitters is not gold, Bob,' I murmured through gritted teeth.

I noticed for the first time too, the thriving transgender community and the flickering, brittle brightness of the bars where they were gathered. It was all new to me. Was this the real reason why Bob had wanted to come to Blackpool? Was this really what he had meant by a new start? A new name and a sex change? How could I have been so blind? So stupid. I was angry with myself.

At first, Bob came with us, every night, to help with the search. We'd hand out leaflets, side by side, mother and father. But then, he began making excuses not to come.

'I'm not sure it's really any use,' he said. 'It's not good for us either. It's destroying you, Karen.'

In truth, he was spending more nights in the pub instead. It would infuriate me as I watched him checking his watch, desperate almost, to escape the house – to escape *us*.

'You should be out there, looking for her!' I shouted. 'You're drinking yourself to death!'

'Let the police do their job, Karen!' he bawled back. 'You're interfering. As usual!'

And with that, he grabbed his wallet and the door slammed. It was his way of shutting off from the trauma, I knew that. But I resented that he could even think of switching off, of looking for relaxation. For me, that was all parcelled up in a past life. And so, with the December nights cold and bitter, I continued my search alone. Emma and Becki came sometimes, and mum was always willing to come too. But I didn't like to put them through it. Mum was old and the girls were vulnerable. I preferred to know they were home – and safe. Yet sometimes, it felt like I was the only one who was looking for Charlene. The police search seemed to have petered out already. I felt like my daughter was being forgotten, shoved aside as 'unfinished paperwork'. I heard from the police once a week, maybe, but I'd make five phone calls before they called me back. It felt as though they just wanted me to give up.

'Why aren't you taking this seriously?' I asked. 'Why aren't you making more effort?'

'We still believe your daughter is a runaway,' insisted the officers. 'We're doing all we can.'

To me, it was clear that they were not. It was so frustrating; I began to think we were being side-lined because of who we were – or weren't. We didn't have good jobs or standing in the community, we were not well respected or well heeled. We had no money, no influence. No, we were a troubled, dysfunctional, chaotic family. I was on the verge of an emotional meltdown. Our kids played up at school. My husband was almost always in the pub. If there was such a thing as the right CV to be taken seriously when a child goes missing, we were woefully lacking. And so, I was left fighting for her all on my own. Uneducated, unpolished and unashamedly working class, but I didn't love my daughter any less for it.

I set about trying to persuade the *Blackpool Gazette*, our local newspaper, to run a story. Day after day, I called the newsdesk, pleading with them to listen.

'Our hands are tied,' explained the news editor. 'The police don't want us to run anything, I'm sorry.'

I wrote to Granada Reports, our local TV station, too. But they said the same, in a polite letter. When I opened the reply, I sighed angrily and screwed it up – it felt like a conspiracy. I nagged and nagged our liaison officer, day after day, for publicity. And six weeks on, mid-December, the local paper finally agreed to run an article.

'It will be an appeal to her, as a runaway, to come home,' the reporter explained. 'That's the police line.'

It wasn't what I had in mind, but at least it was publicity. And I was grateful.

'My Charlene loved Darren Day. Do you think we could ask him to be involved as well?' I suggested. 'People will sit up and take notice of him.'

The *Gazette* contacted him and thankfully, he agreed. As soon as the paper was on sale, at 4pm the next day, I hurried out to the shop to buy a copy. And there, on the front page, was Charlene's photo, next to a headline from Darren Day, pleading: 'Charlene, Come Home!'

'Front page,' said the newsagent, handing me my change. 'That's good news, Mrs Downes.'

I gulped and nodded. I had expected to be pleased when I saw the article, but seeing Charlene's name in black and white sent a chill through me. The stark reality of her disappearance hit me all over again. I walked home, trembling, my heart pounding.

'I don't like seeing her in the paper,' I told Mum. 'It makes me panic more.'

I had pleaded with the newspaper to take it seriously. And now that they had, I was devastated. I had to acknowledge it now, we all did. But I knew the story might bring answers, it might even bring Charlene home. I called our liaison officer and the newspaper offices the next morning, eager for updates.

'Nothing,' they both said. 'Nobody has come forward … Yet …'

I tried not to be too despondent, but the newspaper pages inevitably became the next day's chip wrappers – and the day after that those same pages were blowing along the streets, onto the pier, and into the gutters, alongside my missing posters. The next day and the next, there was no news from the appeal, only more sympathy. And I'd had just about as many hugs and flowers and kind empty words as I could take. I was a mother; drowning, choking, struggling against a tide of disinterest. She was my Charlene, my Babby. I had birthed her, nursed her, put plasters on her grazes, wiped away her tears. I had taught her long division, sung her lullabies, bought her first bra. She was so much a part of me that I felt my own life, without her, was worthless. And even sleep brought fresh agonies: I had more dreams, where I'd see her as a little girl, maybe nine or ten years old.

'Mummy,' she would say, with the widest of smiles, and my bruised heart would sing and shatter all at the same time. And she would reach out to me, her eyes and her mouth still beaming. The love was shining out of her. But as my hand stretched out to hers, I was suddenly, brutally, awake. Now, I was sweating, panic coursing through my veins. Was it worth those few moments of heavenly happiness to be slapped so viciously with the horror of reality every time I awoke? I wanted to sleep, to see Charlene again. But most nights, I lay awake, hour after agonising hour. I'd imagine she was bound, gagged, tortured by an evil gang. I could almost hear her screaming for me. Was she trapped in the dark? It preyed on my mind. Charlene needed a sliver of a light, a glimmer of hope.

Please don't keep her in the dark, I begged silently.

I couldn't even sleep in the dark myself. I kept a bedside light on in her room. Mum didn't mind; she understood. At night, we'd pray together. Though I'd been brought up as a churchgoer, my faith had taken a back seat whilst I was busy raising the children. But now, I was grasping whatever promise – or false promise – came my way. Burying my head in Charlene's pillow, I would plead to God, weeping unashamedly, for some news of my daughter. Surely, he wouldn't desert me now? The Virgin Mary knew what it was to suffer as a mother; she had seen her child die on the cross. And if Charlene was being crucified, right in front of me, my pain could not have been worse.

'Please help me, Mary,' I whispered.

As a little girl, I had never missed Sunday service. I sang in the church choir and Mum was a Sunday School teacher.

'God will always listen,' she had told me. 'He can grant any wish he likes.'

And so, I grew up thinking that God would, or could, sort out anything – no matter what the mess was. When the children were little, I'd tuck them in bed and whisper: 'Please, God, keep them safe from harm.'

Now, I repeated the same prayer – but in desperation, in despair.

'Please, God, keep Charlene safe from harm – wherever she is.'

Each word was heavy with significance. I half-expected to hear a thunder clap or a roar from the heavens in reply. But there was nothing. Was He listening? Night after night, my faith was tested to the very brink, but it was something to cling to. I needed a life raft, though this one was sinking. And I felt that fate had his foot on my head, kicking me under, as my face disappeared beneath the surface. At the end of our street there was a tiny chapel, with a soup kitchen for the homeless. One afternoon, I found myself wandering inside to pray. The volunteers there knew only too well what had happened to Charlene and they knelt with me and we prayed together.

'You're not on your own, Karen,' they told me. 'We pray for you every day.'

It was a comfort. I grasped on to that, yet the days were hard.

And they grew harder.

CHAPTER TEN
CHRISTMAS SPIRIT

That first Christmas, without Charlene, was truly unbearable. Even though I was so distracted, I was painfully aware of the build-up. In a town like Blackpool, it was impossible not to notice the tacky decorations and multi-coloured lights flashing from every hotel, shop and tourist attraction. Normally, I would have loved this, but now, it threw me into total panic. How on earth could I get through it without my daughter? Worse still, how would my other children survive? I left all preparations to the last minute, hoping against hope that Charlene might come home and be our very own Christmas miracle.

The week before Christmas, with time running out, I wrapped her presents, bought weeks before she went missing, and put them under the tree. By now, she had been missing for almost two months and I built myself up, in Christmas week, into believing that she would be home for Christmas Day – perhaps because the alternative was just too painful. I had bought her, Becki and Emma a new pair of Rockport boots each. I'd started saving months earlier so that I could afford the expense when it came.

Come home, darling, I pleaded silently. *Your presents are here and we miss you so much.*

As a little girl, Charlene had always loved Christmas, opening up Barbie dolls and a new bike one year. The memory of her face, lit up with excitement on Christmas morning, was strong in my mind. Then there was the year when she was chosen to sing 'Silent Night' in German at the school Nativity. She was brimming with excitement. I knew she had a lovely voice, so sweet, but she couldn't speak a word of German. She practised, night after night, until she was word perfect. And watching that concert was one of the proudest moments of my life; it made my Christmas. Mum came along with me, because Bob couldn't get the time off work.

'That's my daughter,' I whispered to the parents next to me as Charlene took to the stage. 'That's my Charlene, you know.'

Charlene loved going carol singing too. She and Martin would go out, door to door, singing Christmas songs. The previous year, they had taken Robert along with them too. After collecting the money for charity, a few kind members of the public also gave them some small change for their efforts. Charlene spent hers on buying gifts for the rest of us. The festivities had always been such a happy time when the children were young: expensive, exhausting and stressful – but wonderful, nonetheless. Bob would go mad with Christmas cheer – lights inside and out, dancing reindeer on the hearth, blow-up snowmen on the roof. He was like a big kid, he went overboard. We'd see him stuck up a step ladder on the front path, a knot of Christmas lights around his neck, bawling for one of us to go outside and help him, which we never did.

'Dad's at it again!' Becki would laugh.

The kids would peer out of the window, hoping he'd fall off his ladder and make them laugh even more. The atmosphere was lovely; wholesome, warm. On Christmas Eve the children would snuggle up and watch *The Muppet Christmas Carol* on TV or Charlene's favourite, *Aladdin*. They liked to watch *Snow White* too and would tease their nanna that she looked just like the wicked Peddler.

'You horrible children!' she screeched, doing a perfect impression, and the kids would giggle and run to hide behind the couch. It was cosy, happy … safe. This Christmas, by stark contrast, could not have been more agonising. The kids didn't want to celebrate. They didn't send cards. They wouldn't help Bob decorate the Christmas tree. He cut a forlorn, broken figure as he plonked the plastic tree in the corner of the living room, like some unwanted intruder. I spotted a solitary tear, rolling slowly down his cheek, as he switched on the fairy lights.

'I wish she was here,' he said quietly.

I felt an awful sadness well up inside me. I wanted to reach out to Bob – to let him know I understood his suffering – but I couldn't. My own was too much for me to bear. And so, I had to leave him to manage alone. Emma and Becki would usually have an extortionate list of teenage demands at Christmas. In years gone by, I'd had sleepless nights about how I'd be able to afford the perfume and make-up and expensive clothes they were asking for. One Christmas, I had bought the same silver hooped earrings for them both, a fatal mistake.

'I don't want to wear the same as her!' Becki grumbled.

'Neither do I!' Emma shrieked.

The argument rumbled on, and as I dressed the turkey in the kitchen, I heard them brawling in the living room. Mum appeared at the doorway a few minutes later, breathless.

'I had to pull them apart,' she told me, 'all over a pair of earrings!'

I smiled – it was all part of growing up. But I had learned my lesson and never bought them matching presents ever again. Now, I'd have given the world to have such trivial worries. Yet this year, the girls asked for nothing.

'Just Charlene,' said Becki sadly. 'We want our sister back.'

I had no heart to celebrate either. But I knew it was important – for their sakes and for our family's sanity – to carry on.

On Christmas morning, the kids raced downstairs to open their presents, for a moment caught up in the festive excitement, but then their faces fell.

'Didn't Santa bring Charlene back?' Robert asked angrily.

In the simplicity of a 12 year old's world, Santa could solve anything, grant any wish. He felt cheated. This was the first year Santa had let him down. Meanwhile, the girls fretted and became tearful.

'Let's wait,' Emma suggested. 'She might show up. We could all open our gifts together.'

But the waiting was unbearable. By late morning, holding back tears, they opened their presents alone. Still hopeful, I set her a place at the dinner table. I peeled enough potatoes for six and rolled extra pigs in blankets – just in case. We ate in strained silence, staring at her chair, her empty place, the leftover food. The silence was so painful. But by evening, I could take no more. I ripped off my Christmas party hat and sobbed. Little Robert and his sisters were bewildered. How could the world celebrate when Charlene was missing? Fairy lights twinkled at every window. Families laughed, ate, drank, argued.

Together. And my Charlene was out there – somewhere – on her own.

So much for Christmas wishes, I told myself bitterly.

Hope, I had learned, could be a dangerous thing. It was the hope that crushed you. Sucked out your spirit. Spat you out. And yet you kept on going back for more. Because without hope, there really was nothing at all.

CHAPTER ELEVEN
WANDERING THE STREETS

Coping with my own grief was one thing, but seeing my children struggle was, if it's possible, even worse. I watched their personalities, the very fabric of who they were, become dismantled and destroyed. It was as though they had two lives, separated by Charlene disappearing: one before, one after. Emma had been a really giggly girl – she loved dancing and she adored her dolls. She was a good swimmer too, the only one of my children who could swim well. And she was a talented artist. Quite often, she would sit and draw for hours at the dining table. I'd buy her sketch pads and coloured pencils for every birthday. She was thoughtful and reflective; responsible and mature too. As our eldest child, she naturally looked out for her little sisters and brother. I knew I could rely on her.

Becki was a completely different kettle of fish: loud, feisty and full of confidence. And as she grew older, she preferred Power Rangers to dolls.

'I'm the pink Power Ranger!' she would shout, throwing herself off the couch, shooting us all dead with the kitchen brush handle.

And she grew up more quickly than Emma; she liked going out with her mates after school. And so did Charlene. Off they'd go, arm in arm, down to the shops or to the arcades. I gave them £5 each and it was like gold dust in their little hands. They were carefree, innocent, just as children should be. But Charlene's disappearance smashed everything apart. The girls seemed to grow up, literally in the space of a few days. Lines appeared on their faces, their eyes heavy with worry. They carried a burden no child should ever have to bear. But they kept themselves busy, searching, tracking down Charlene's friends, asking around their own friends and frantically tapping out the same text messages to anyone who might have seen her. They went out searching too, often going out with Bob and tramping the streets around our home. Yet I was terrified of letting them leave the house, convinced I would lose them as well.

'Stay where I can see you,' I pleaded. 'Leave the searching to us.'

But they wouldn't hear of it.

'We need to join in,' they insisted. 'We want to help.'

And I knew they would have more idea of where Charlene might be – she was sure to have shared gossip with them that she would never tell me. And yet, they seemed just as shocked and bewildered as I was.

'Mum, Charlene is still just a little girl,' they said. 'She had no secrets, not that we know.'

In their shared room Becki and Emma both had 'Take That' bedspreads and posters on the wall. Their CDs were scattered on the carpet, there were sweet wrappers by the beds. But when I went in one day to tidy round, it hit me, with a whack, that they had suddenly outgrown all this, all this teenage frivolity and fun. Instantly, they were adults now in an adult world. These bedcovers and posters no longer seemed appropriate – their childhoods had ended the moment their sister skipped off out the door. I worried so much that they were taking on too much stress, but how could they avoid it?

'We just want Charlene home,' they told me. 'We'll do whatever it takes.'

Robert was only 12 years old and because he was our baby – and the only boy out of the four – he was spoiled and mollycoddled even more. Emma and Becki made such a fuss of him, and so did I. Robert was a typical little boy; he loved tearing around the house, playing tag. He liked kicking a football around with his mates in the street outside our home; he adored Liverpool FC. It caused huge ructions with Charlene, who declared herself a Manchester United fan just to wind him up. The two of them would argue and bicker like mad on derby days. Robert dreamed of being a footballer himself when he grew up. He had the same dreams as every other little boy. And he loved superheroes too – Spider-Man and Batman. Often, he'd play quite happily, in a world of his own, with his little superhero figures. He rarely thought beyond what he was having for his tea that night and worried only about Liverpool's match results. At first, I managed to protect him from much of what was going on, but as the days passed, he began to ask for his sister.

'When's she coming home?' he wondered. 'Where has she gone?'

I shrugged, helplessly: there were no answers. The police searched our house and Robert was farmed out to neighbours and friends to try and shield him from the upset. When Bob was interviewed, I tried to reassure Robert, but it wasn't easy – he could sense the worry and the tension in our house. The air was thick with it; stress hung like a toxic smog in every room. Bob and I, far from exchanging our usual trivial niggles and clashing at flashpoints, barely spoke. And much of the abuse he heard at the pub was repeated to Robert in the schoolyard. The other children were cruel, unspeakably so.

'The other kids are saying Dad knows where Charlene is,' Robert told me, his eyes wide with confusion and fear. 'What do they mean? One boy told me that Dad killed Charlene.'

Robert wanted to defend his dad; stand up for his sister. And he got into trouble at school, fighting with the children who had teased him about Charlene. He was angry, scared and lashing out at whoever was in his way.

'What can I do?' I snapped, when his teachers called me. 'What do you expect? He's just a child, he shouldn't have to deal with this.'

Late one night, there was a rap at the door and I found an officer – with little Robert – standing outside. I was baffled – I'd tucked Robert up in bed hours earlier, I had thought that was where he was now. I checked my watch and it was 2:30am.

'What are you doing there?' I asked Robert, eventually finding my voice.

He fidgeted nervously but said nothing.

'We found your son wandering around,' said the officer grimly. 'He's only a little boy, he shouldn't be walking the streets at this hour.'

'I thought he was asleep in bed,' I said faintly. 'I'm so sorry, I really am.'

The officer went, and Robert stumbled into the house, tears streaming down his cheeks.

'Where have you been?' I demanded. 'What on earth are you playing at?'

'I've been out looking for Charlene,' he sobbed, clenching his fists in frustration. 'I want my sister, I want to bring her home.'

My heart dropped like a stone. Horrified, I listened as Robert explained he had been climbing out his window, night after night, and wandering the streets alone. He'd pulled on a pair of tracksuit bottoms and his coat, and gone off, into the darkness. I hadn't even noticed. I hadn't heard him leave. I hadn't seen his empty bed. I hadn't heard his cries. Since Charlene had gone, I had felt I could take no more emotion. Yet I was swamped by guilt and self-reproach. What kind of mother was I? I had one child missing, another walking the streets. I was so focussed on Charlene that I had neglected my other children. I'd been so busy listening to my own heart breaking that I hadn't heard Robert's breaking too – I was failing him. My family was breaking up, piece by piece.

'Oh, Trebor,' I said, taking him in my arms, 'please don't ever do this again, it's dangerous.'

It was frightening even to think of him climbing down the drainpipe. But then for him to be roaming the same town, the same streets, where Charlene had disappeared ...

'You can't do it,' I repeated, more desperately than before. 'It's a miracle you've not been hurt yet.'

But he was defiant.

'I need to find her,' he said. 'I won't stop looking, she's my sister.'

Then he screwed up his fists again and I knew he meant it. Filled with tension and aggression, he needed an outlet.

'You and I can look for her together,' I compromised. 'But you must not go alone.'

The next night, and the next, I had to check on him, every hour or so, to stop him sneaking out. I was like a prison officer, it was horrible. Sometimes I'd tiptoe in and out, every few minutes, unable to take my eyes off him. I'd spend the whole night pacing up and down. But though he was there, in bed, I was losing him; I could feel it, he was becoming angrier and more withdrawn. I noticed, even when he slept, his little fists were clenched tightly. At school, his teachers were struggling to cope. If anyone mentioned Charlene's name, Robert would explode with rage. He threw a chair at a boy, who had taunted him that Charlene was dead. He floored another with a punch.

'He's off the rails,' said his teacher.

'We're *all* off the rails,' I said bitterly. 'All of us.'

Inevitably, early in the New Year of 2004, social services got in touch. They were concerned, they said, that I couldn't cope with Robert.

Too right, I can't cope! I wanted to scream. *Who could?*

But I knew what would happen if I was honest with

them: Robert would be taken away. And I wouldn't – *couldn't* – lose another child. And so, I agreed quietly.

'I'd really appreciate any help you can offer,' I told them. 'It's a difficult time for us.'

The social workers meant well; they made an appointment to come and see us. Before they arrived, I scrubbed the house obsessively, worried dirty pots in the sink might be a sign I wasn't up to the job of looking after my son. I perched on the couch, answering every question, nodding enthusiastically to every suggestion. I hoped that might be the end of it, but the following week they came back, again by appointment, but I knew I had no choice but to comply.

'We need to be sure Robert is OK,' they explained.

Bob was surly, unfriendly. But mum, like me, thought it was best to get along with them.

'They're only doing their job,' she said.

Even so, they swarmed in and out of our home and I couldn't get rid of them – it was like having an ants' nest in the fridge. They'd call and see us, just for a coffee, but really, I knew they were watching every move I made.

'I don't like them coming round my house,' Bob complained. 'They make me feel uncomfortable.'

'Well, go out then,' I snapped. 'Because there's nothing we can do about it.'

The social workers were here to stay. And so, we plastered over the gaping wound in our family and we hobbled on. Emma had been working in the café at BHS when Charlene went missing and Becki then got a job in an office. But afterwards, neither of them could carry on with their day-to-day routine. They had more and more time off work and though they tried to return, it was as their new selves, not the old ones. And they just didn't fit in any more. One day, one of Emma's workmates made a comment about Charlene and she snapped, ripping off her apron and marching out.

'I'm not going back,' she said. 'I can't take it. My head is spinning with all this, Mum. People keep asking me about Charlene, I can't stand it.'

And the same happened with Becki. She had been doing so well at work, her boss had been really pleased with her. But she was unable to concentrate; she couldn't sit at a desk.

'I think about Charlene all the time,' she told me.

I worried terribly about them both, but I didn't want their lives ruined too. I encouraged them to go out, with their pals, as all teenagers should. Keeping them at home, night after night, wasn't the answer; it wasn't fair on them. Yet on the rare occasion they ventured out, they couldn't even relax.

'I look for Charlene constantly,' Emma told me. 'Every bar, every takeaway, every arcade … I search for her all the time. I keep thinking I might see her, down a back alley, or in the back of some dingy pub.'

And yet, of the three, it was Becki who carried the biggest weight of her sister's disappearance. She blamed herself, purely because she'd been with Charlene the night she disappeared.

'If I'd insisted on her coming home with me, she'd still be here today.'

She'd say it over and over again, tormenting herself. It was irrational and illogical, but she was eaten up with guilt and regret.

'I should never have left her,' she sobbed. 'It's my fault.'

People would quiz her about Charlene and whisper behind her back. Even well-meaning comments would leave her in tears. I was so worried about her, I took her to the GP and she received counselling. But nothing really helped.

'What's the point of seeing a counsellor?' she asked helplessly. 'It won't bring Charlene home.'

Little Robert, 13 now, was spiralling out of control. He got into fights outside school, each one more violent than the last, and soon he was in trouble with the police too. We had police officers knocking on our door, looking for him, telling us he had been picking fights and attacking strangers.

'This isn't how I brought him up,' I told them. 'He really is not that sort of boy.'

I didn't want to make excuses for him but, as a teenager, his life had been dominated by the search for Charlene. He hadn't been violent before she went missing. In fact, he'd always been a rather happy-go-lucky, mild sort of kid.

'I can't handle it,' he told me.

'I know, son,' I said.

It was no real surprise, yet no less of a disappointment, when Robert was thrown out of school and moved to a specialist unit in Lancaster. A minibus came to collect him, every morning, and he was given a dark-blue tracksuit to wear instead of his school uniform. At the new place, he went fishing and walking and he relaxed more than I'd seen in months. He learned how to calm his temper a little. But there was no getting away from it: Charlene's disappearance had ruined his life completely, changed the course of who he would become and what kind of man he would be. It was a tragedy that threw up fresh, raw heartbreak every day: my children were not the same people they had once been. By turns, they had become angry and aggressive or inward-looking and depressive. Like head lice, the social services buzzed in and out of our home just as they pleased. Yet I knew what power they held and so, I did exactly as they said. Bob and I had the same old conversations, over and over again. He made it seem like it was my fault that the social workers were round all the time.

'I hate them, poking round my house,' he complained.

'We've no choice,' I reminded him. 'We've just got to accept it, that's the way things are. Besides,' – and I was irritable now – 'we need help with Robert. I don't know how to help him, do you?'

At this Bob looked mildly surprised, as though Robert's problems were nothing to do with him. And to me, that was all the more reason to let the social workers into our lives. But I knew he was simmering. One day, in February 2004, a social worker visited – a nice young woman, with long, fair hair. She stood in the kitchen and gave us a friendly smile before putting her files down on the side of the sink.

'We want to try to keep Robert at home, with you both,' she began tentatively, 'and so we'd like you to sign an agreement, which confirms your commitment to working with us.'

'Yes, of course,' I agreed.

I didn't even hesitate; I was so desperate. Besides, what was so wrong with wanting to keep our son on the straight and narrow? But from behind me, Bob suddenly exploded, banging his fists on the kitchen table.

'No, I won't sign your f***ing agreement!' he bawled. 'How dare you come in here, telling me what to do with my own son! How bloody *dare* you!'

Incensed, he looked around wildly and picked up the first thing he spotted – a bag of potatoes. Eyes blazing, he towered over her, like some sort of second-rate Hulk. The poor girl fled, screaming, as he hurled the whole bag after her. I stood staring, horrified and appalled.

'Are you OK?' I called, rushing outside after her. But she had gone, leaving just a few stray papers fluttering in the street. Back in the house, I rounded on Bob, my temper raging. The bag had split and there were potatoes rolling all over the floor.

'Why did you do that?' I demanded. 'Why did you attack that poor woman? She was terrified.'

'I don't like social workers,' he replied.

'Neither do I,' I snapped. 'But throwing potatoes at the social worker is just like throwing them at yourself. At your own son. This will come back on us, on little Robert. You see if it doesn't.'

Bob snorted. But I saw a flicker of panic shoot across his face.

'They can't do anything to Robert,' he bragged, sounding louder and brasher than he felt.

I burst into tears. After all I had been through – the meetings with school, the police, social services. I had been patient and agreeable, reasonable and rational; I had bitten my tongue on so many occasions. And it was all to keep Robert with us, at home, and out of care. But Bob had chucked all my hard work away in a moment of self-indulgent madness. I felt such anger towards him, such loathing, that it frightened me. That same evening, at 6pm, a male social worker knocked on the door. My legs buckled as I spotted a police officer standing next to him.

'Can we speak with your son, Robert, please?' asked the social worker.

'Why?' I asked warily.

'We are worried he might be at risk from his father,' said the social worker bluntly.

'You're taking him into care?' I asked weakly.

The silence said it all. My head was swimming. I felt the energy drain from me, as if I was no longer strong enough even to stand up.

Another child gone, said a voice in my head.

Was this some sort of ghoulish family tradition?

'He's not here,' I said, quite truthfully.

Robert was out with a pal. The social worker agreed to return the following morning and I promised, biting back tears, I'd have him back for then. But as soon as the door closed, I called a close family friend named John and asked him to look after Robert for me overnight. I knew it was wrong. For the first time in my life, I had disobeyed the social workers, I had gone against the system. But I didn't see what else I could do.

The following morning, I went to see a solicitor.

'You have to let them take him,' he advised. 'You'll get into all sorts of trouble otherwise. You've no choice.'

Sobbing, I made my way home. I couldn't bear to tell Robert, my little Trebor. He was my baby and I had failed him. I gave the social workers John's address and they went there to take him. Robert screamed and sobbed; they had to virtually drag him to the car. Watching outside, I collapsed, anguished, and in that instant, I wanted to die: not one, but two children gone. The car drove away, with Robert's tear-stained face pressed against the back window, looking out helplessly at the life he was leaving behind. My grief fast burning up into rage, I marched home to confront Bob.

'This is your fault!' I screamed. '*Yours!*'

He looked startled, as though I was being unreasonable.

'You had better stay out of my way,' I seethed. 'Go to the pub, as you always do. And don't come back.'

That night, the social worker called me. I was frantic for news.

'Where is he?' I pleaded. 'Is he OK?'

He explained that Robert had been taken to a children's home in Manchester, an hour's drive away. That seemed like the final twist of the knife. He was miles and miles away – out there, in the darkness, just like his sister. I was still sobbing when Bob came home from the pub, hours later, stony-faced.

'I am not having those bastards telling me what to do,' he slurred stubbornly.

'So, where does that leave Robert? And me?' I wept.

'What about you?' he snarled, as if I was a mere afterthought.

And really, that said it all: that was how he felt.

'I won't ever forgive you,' I said coldly. '*Ever.*'

CHAPTER TWELVE
WAITING BY THE WINDOW

It felt very final. Bob had given me a son. And now, it was his fault that I had lost him. After 16 years of marriage, I was nothing more than an afterthought for him. We were so far apart. Wounded and damaged. In those early days – it was unthinkable now – he'd made me feel so special. When we were dating, we went out for nice meals and Bob would always pick up the bill – he was such a gentleman. That first year, after we met, he booked tickets for us to see Michael Barrymore's Christmas show. He had bought me a big bottle of Panache perfume. He wasn't an overly generous or affectionate man, and of course he didn't have a lot of money to spare, but somehow it all made those little gifts count all the more. Then I'd fallen pregnant with Emma and it was a surprise to us both. Yet we were pleased and Bob hadn't faltered at all.

'I'll look after you both,' he promised. 'I won't let you down. I'll make you proud of me, Karen.'

Naively, I'd seen his words as a show of strength, of manliness. But looking back, it was another sign of the vulnerability that had come into such sharp focus after his alter ego as Martina was exposed. He was desperate to please me – to prove himself – as though he was the child and I was the parent. Had I cared about him more than I had loved him? But back then, I had been too busy shopping for prams, worrying about stretch marks and choosing baby names to overanalyse our relationship.

The pregnancy went well and I bloomed; I loved having a bump. Bob was good around the house – decorating the baby's room, fixing the cot together, wiring up a night light. I was good at homemaking, the nesting – I paid all the bills, answered all the letters, did the washing, ironing and cooking. We made a good team and I didn't look beyond that.

When Emma was two years old, I'd said to him, when he came home from work, 'How do you fancy getting married one day?'

Bob's face had lit up. When I thought back to it now, he was like a little boy being given a present or a day out he'd been longing for. He had wanted to belong. To fit in. He wanted to get married. And much more than that, he had wanted to know that I wanted to marry him.

'I'm game if you are.' He beamed. 'I can't bloody wait!'

Mum had whooped when she heard the news, but said: 'You will always be my daughter, Karen. I won't ever lose you.'

I wore a long white dress and had six bridesmaids, for our wedding at St Peter's Church, Coventry, on May 2 1987. Emma was one of my bridesmaids, as was my best pal, Lorraine. She was Emma's godmother too. At the door to the church, my dad joked: 'You can still change your mind, Karen!'

But I giggled and shook my head. I had no doubts at all. And the reason I felt so certain was because I felt sure of who Bob was and what he offered. And now, all of that had been thrown up in the air and landed, smashed, on the ground. I'd thought he was a devoted husband – and yet he secretly wanted to be a woman. I'd thought he was a devoted father too – yet now his son was in care and it was all his fault. On the night of our wedding, our flat was burgled: the TV and video player were stolen and the whole place was ransacked.

'What a start to married life!' Bob had sighed, sweeping up shards of broken glass, still in his wedding suit.

Yes, what a start! Over the years, during our many rows and disagreements, I would pull my wedding ring off in a fit of temper and fling it across the room. It hit the wall so many times that it became dented and scratched and the shine was dulled. Every time I looked at it, I'd be reminded of the rows we'd had. Now, with Robert gone, I ripped it from my finger and it rolled, sadly, across the room. I knew I'd never wear it again.

The following morning, I had to go to the family court. And it was in a cold, impersonal room, with Formica furniture and strip lighting, that little Robert was officially lost. I was told I would be allowed to visit him every two weeks, as though I was nothing more than a distant aunt. The days dragged until my first visit. Bob stayed at home, and Mum and I went by train, with the tickets booked and paid for by the social services. As we waited on the platform, shivering in the wind, she smiled and said: 'I can't wait to see him.'

But I felt sick inside; I was almost frightened of going to see my own son. The formality of the occasion was daunting. I took him chocolates and new clothes but they seemed poor compensation for the loss of his family and his home. We had arranged with his care worker to meet in a café, near the children's home. The moment he saw me, Robert threw himself at me.

'Mum, take me home,' he sobbed. 'Please!'

It tore me apart. I had so much to say, there was so much I needed to tell him, that I ended up saying nothing at all.

'I think you've grown!' was all I managed.

The visit was awkward, with a care worker hovering nearby. And I wasn't used to having sit-down enforced chats with my own son. I didn't want to sit stiffly across a table from him, I wanted him to loll on the sofa, drop crumbs out of his crisp packet, surf the TV channels, until I lost patience with him – I wanted things back to how they were. Mum did her best to fill in the silences, asking him if he liked the food and if he had a comfy bed. But her voice was small and cracking with emotion. Leaving him was worse than I could have imagined, he sobbed and shouted again, crying out like an injured animal. I wanted to lie down and cry with him. But I knew, as his mum, I had to try to be strong.

'I'll be back soon,' I promised, swallowing my tears.

The train journey home was utterly miserable; the fields and trees and towns whizzed by, all through a blur of my tears, and each station we stopped at only served to accentuate how far I was away from him.

'He may as well be on the other side of the world,' I wept.

Mum gave my arm a comforting pat, but I could tell she was crying too. And if I thought time would help, I was wrong – each visit seemed worse than the one before. Bob came with me sometimes, but the atmosphere was strained. Robert blamed him, as I did; he was an angry young man and Bob bore the brunt of his fury many times. I could understand that. But I never missed a single visit and Robert and I stayed close.

'I miss you, Mum,' he told me. 'Why can't I come home?'

'I'm doing my best,' I said helplessly. 'I'm fighting for you, I keep asking social services.'

The manager of the home was so kind to us. He'd call me, during the week, to let me know how Robert was doing (he had stayed at the same school, which was a couple of hours' drive each way, but at least there was one constant in his life). In the evenings, he took Robert to watch stock car racing or out to play football. But Robert was still fighting, still getting into bother. He'd disappear out of his bedroom window, after lights out, and go out looking for trouble. Yet the social workers still insisted that he was better off in care.

'We have to do what is best for the child, Mrs Downes,' they said.

Grief-stricken, defeated, I had to accept that fortnightly visits with my son would be the nearest I got to being his mother for a long time to come. And yet it reached the stage where I dreaded going to see him, because I couldn't bear to leave him at the end of our two hours together. Saying goodbye was such a painful wrench – it felt as though someone was tearing my whole body in two. And each time, the scab was ripped off again, more viciously, more painfully, than the time before.

On those occasions when Bob came with me, we barely spoke on the train. I made little effort to disguise how much I despised him. Charlene's bed was empty, Robert's bed was empty: my Babby and my Trebor, both stolen from me. Each night, I'd cry myself to sleep in Charlene's bed.

'I hate you for this!' I spat at Bob. 'And I will always hate you.'

Bob stared at me in shock. But he said nothing. I was alarmed by the loathing I felt for him – I had never dreamt I was capable of such hatred. Was this the new me, was this the new normal? For gradually, much as I railed against it, life did return to some sort of chaotic routine as the spring of 2004 began.

Then Emma announced she was moving out and she got her own flat nearby. She got a job as a dancer in one of the Blackpool clubs, which would just about cover the rent. And though the flat was small, it was cosy and clean.

'It's time I moved on, Mum,' she said.

Part of me was proud of her; she was a strong girl, forging a path through life despite her pain. But I felt a sense of bereavement too, as if I was losing another one of my chicks. I worried that something might happen to her too, especially working late in the nightclub. Under my wing, I had felt more able to protect her from the dark malevolence that I now knew ran like sewage through the streets of Blackpool. Now, out on her own, I felt she was vulnerable. Like Charlene.

A couple of months later, Becki decided to leave too, unable to cope with the constant reminders of her little sister.

'I see her in every room,' she told me. 'I can feel her around me and it tears me to bits, I can't stand being in this house.'

She went to stay with Emma. And it was good for them to be together, I knew that. They'd become fiercely close since Charlene had gone and I was in no doubt that they would look after each other. And I didn't want them dragged down by me and Bob: shuffling through life, waiting, always waiting. I bought them a new dinner set, as a housewarming, and they invited me round for tea. Emma was a wonderful cook; she had always been able to rustle up a meal without a problem, even at primary school. She liked good, solid food like shepherd's pie and spaghetti Bolognese. When I went, that first time, she made a big stew.

'Delicious, Emma.' I smiled.

Becki was the complete opposite. I remembered her once saying she was going to fry an egg, and she chucked it in the pan with the shell on! But whilst Emma was the chef, Becki was a natural homemaker. Emma was a real flibbertigibbet, very untidy and messy; Becki was tidy and methodical.

'Between you two girls, you make a good team.' I smiled.

They still came home three or four times a week too. One night, Emma popped in with a DVD of a film called *The Lovely Bones*.

'Watch this, Mum,' she said. 'It will make you cry.'

And as I settled down to watch it, I realised, with a start, what she meant. The film was about a young girl (Susie Salmon) who had been murdered. Nobody knew what had happened to her – and it was told through her own dead voice. The young actress who played her (Saoirse Ronan) bore such an uncanny resemblance to Charlene, it took my breath away. I wept as I watched it. And just outside the window, through the curtains, I fancied I heard a whooshing sound – a spirit dancing, giggling, down our street?

'What did you think?' Emma asked, the next time I saw her.

'It gave me the jitters,' I told her truthfully.

I knew it had unsettled Emma too. And I invited her and Becki for lunch that Sunday – I wanted to keep an eye on them both. They started coming every weekend and they'd bring their dirty washing or a coat that needed new buttons.

'It's not a bloody launderette!' Bob would shriek when he saw the clothes piled high by the washing machine. But the next minute, he'd have his arms around them –

he missed them too, just as I did. When they left again, carrying food parcels and bags of clean clothes, the house was eerily quiet. And the sense of loss was all-consuming. The grief seemed to drag me down physically. With all of my children gone, I felt that the act I had put on, for their sakes, had outlived its purpose: my audience had all gone. And so, like an old has-been luvvie, following a last, pathetic show on the pier, I allowed myself to crumble. I was too tired to wash my hair; I wore the same clothes, day after day. It seemed an over-facing, just to tidy the house. My limbs felt so heavy, I could hardly get out of bed. And when I did make it downstairs in the morning, I'd find last night's dishes in the sink. That would have been unthinkable before. I had always been very house-proud; it was a constant, thankless task, cleaning up after four kids, but I would never have gone to bed and left the kitchen untidy – it wasn't my way. Now, the dirty dishes hardly registered with me.

'The milk's been left out of the fridge all night,' Bob complained. 'It's probably gone off now. No cereal then.'

In his way, he was doubtless drowning in depression too. He didn't seem able, or willing, to go to the shop and buy more. I shrugged; I wasn't interested anyway. As always, Mum helped. She'd pop out to the corner shop for supplies. She'd scurry around the kitchen like a busy squirrel whilst I slumped on a chair, in my pyjamas, looking aimlessly out of the window. Just in case. Mum would bring me brews and toast and take my head in her hands when I cried. But she pushed me to carry on, too.

'You have to look after yourself,' she insisted. 'Have a shower, put some clean clothes on. When did you last run a brush through your hair?'

That spring of 2004, Mum made a doctor's appointment and came with me. The GP listened sympathetically and gave me sedatives and antidepressants. I took the tablets obediently, mechanically, but knowing nothing would really help: a missing child is a terminal condition. And what was the chance of a miracle cure? As the days passed, the medication kicked in and the panic was dulled. But the pain still throbbed. *And anyway*, I thought angrily, *I didn't want it all to go away. I didn't want to feel better. Not until my babies came home.* I knew that sedatives could be addictive, harmful even. But that didn't worry me. I didn't really care about what happened to me. Nothing mattered at all – except my Charlene.

Her posters were still all over town, but it was as if they'd become part of the landscape; nobody noticed her any more. It was as if the whole town – the police included – had taken sedatives just like me. I had no contact from the police, there was no progress. Our liaison officer would return my calls with platitudes and bland reassurances. But her words, designed to bring comfort, only stung. It felt as though Charlene was nobody's priority, nobody's concern. Except mine. Of course Bob and Mum and the kids all loved and missed her. My own grief was so all-consuming that on occasion I was in danger of ignoring their suffering. But as Charlene's mother, I felt a pain so keen and so cruel that I sometimes struggled to breathe through it. It was as if my own life was so closely knitted to hers that I could not exist without her. People still remembered who she was; they would hug me and spit at me alternately, and really, by now, I was quite indifferent to both. But nobody was actually doing anything practical. Charlene was fast becoming a distant memory, like one winter's heavy snowfall or the year everyone had flu at Christmas. She was fading away. Our family – what was left of it – was haemorrhaging; limping on, day by day. Each morning, I would look at Bob and be reminded that Robert was waking up in a strange bed, in a strange house, far from home – because of him. We'd go for days without speaking. I thought about leaving him, but I was too consumed with worry about Charlene and Robert to make any definite plans for myself. Until they were home, all else seemed to blur into insignificance, and that included my marriage and my own happiness. Besides, there was a small part of me, though I would never have admitted it, that still felt something for Bob.

I didn't love him, not after Robert was taken away. But I felt sorry for him and I worried about him. I didn't know how – or if – he'd cope on his own. Besides, I had taken my marriage vows very seriously. I believed my children should have a mother and a father – together. I wanted a close-knit family unit. It sounds laughable now, with the terrible mess we were in, but I felt that Bob and I were the cornerstones and if we stuck together, perhaps everything else would eventually fall into place around us. Was that enough to make a marriage work? Probably not. But it would have to do.

That first Mother's Day, the kids bought cards and signed Charlene's name, along with theirs.

'She'll be thinking of you, Mum,' Emma said gently. 'Wherever she is.'

I did my best to get through the day. I bought my mum a card and a new jumper. She had never been one for flowers and chocolates, she was far too practical for luxuries like that. And she loved her jumper, but she, like me, was struggling to stay strong, for the kids. We didn't celebrate; there seemed no point. Charlene's 15th birthday – in March 2004 – was torture. I bought presents and put money in a card for her. Just like at Christmas, I built myself up into believing she might be home for her birthday. The day passed, quiet and oppressive. I lingered by the window, by now expecting nothing.

'She's not coming, love,' Mum said gently.

But I stayed, looking out onto the street, fixated, unable to look away. Just in case … Bob went to the pub, unable to stand the weight of expectation at home, and the chasm between us grew ever wider. With each occasion that Charlene missed, each of our birthdays, each family event, I became more and more convinced that she was being held, somewhere, against her will. That she wanted to come home – but could not. It was the only rational explanation. If she was a runaway, she'd have been home by now, or at least have been in contact. If not with me, with one of her sisters or her nanna, surely? If she was dead, and I never allowed myself – or rather, could bring myself – to say it out loud, there would have been a body found. I felt, instinctively and logically, that she had been kidnapped. And that fear of her being held in the dark returned to haunt me every night. She was there – bound with dirty rags, her poor hands and feet bleeding, her eyes wide with terror.

'I can sense her,' I told Mum. 'I know she's in danger.'

CHAPTER THIRTEEN
PSYCHIC VISIONS

The agony of half-knowing was worse than not knowing at all. It was like being drip-fed information, snatching at half-clues, grasping at swirling shadows in the dark. Desperate to know more, I arranged to see a psychic, near our home in Blackpool. I'd read about her a few times in the newspaper and she was highly respected. It wasn't really my thing, I had never seen a psychic before. In the past I would probably have laughed and scoffed at the idea. But desperation is very humbling and I was prepared to try anything. If hacking off my own arms and legs would have helped to bring her home, I would have done it myself, without hesitation.

'I'll come with you,' Mum offered. 'It's worth a try, of course it is.'

Bob rolled his eyes when he saw us getting ready. But I wasn't waiting for his approval. I knew better than that. We took along a locket, on a chain, with Charlene's photo inside. The locket had been a present from Mum for a birthday one year – it was so precious to me and I wore it all the time. As the psychic lived nearby, Mum and I walked round there together and I tapped nervously on the door. The lady who answered was small and well dressed, and more business-like than I had expected. I handed over £25 and it seemed suddenly a rather meagre and pathetic sum of money – I felt as though I was offering her a handful of old beans in exchange for the Golden Egg. As Mum and I sat down, I noticed crystal balls, balanced on shelves around the room, and a shiver ran through me. The psychic laid out a set of cards in front of me.

'You've been through great tragedy,' she said immediately.

I nodded. That was, of course, no great revelation – I was sure she must know who I was. She asked if I could give her something that was special to me. And so, I unclasped the locket and passed it to her. As she grasped it, she grimaced and said: 'It's shaking, it's shaking violently, on the inside.'

Then, she took a deep breath and her words cut through me.

'She was stabbed,' she told me. 'I can see the glint of a knife. Her body is in the water, weighed down by bricks.

She's crying out to you – to find her. She's in the dark and she wants you to find her.'

The temperature in the room seemed to plummet. I gasped. This was what I had sensed, this was what I had known: this was my nightmare.

'Where is she?' I demanded.

'It's marshy and boggy.' The psychic frowned. 'It's dark. They cut off her head … Her body is in pieces now … I'm sorry.'

I could take no more. Sobbing in anguish, I ran from her house and out into the brittle welcome of the daylight. I was hardly able to stand up; the shock seemed to have affected my balance. Mum must have followed me out and I felt her grab me under the arms and say: 'I'm here, Karen. I'm here for you.'

Dizzy and disorientated, I gripped her hand all the way home, as if I was a little girl again.

'She's in the dark,' I whispered. 'She needs me. I knew it, I have to find her.'

Mum was weeping, silently, as she cupped my hand in hers. But her reply was cautious.

'Don't accept everything she says, Karen,' she told me. 'We still have to believe that Charlene is alive. We have to believe.'

I knew Mum was right: I had to stay positive. But, over the next few days, I was plagued by images of the hellish picture the psychic had created. A damp, dark, cold prison. A marshy, boggy hole. This was no place for any child, dead or alive. I called the police and begged them to speak to the psychic.

'She says Charlene is in water, in a marshy area,' I told them. 'Will you do a search? Will you speak to her?'

But the police refused to entertain such an idea. I was annoyed – it wasn't as if they had any leads themselves and Charlene had been missing almost a year.

'What's the harm in just hearing what she has to say?' I demanded.

It was so frustrating. The year anniversary of Charlene's disappearance was fast approaching and my anxiety at getting through another milestone was all-consuming. I called the local paper and they agreed, a little more easily this time, to run another appeal. Charlene's photo appeared on TV too. I put up more posters and gave out more leaflets, but I was losing faith.

No, I told myself firmly, *you, of all people, must have hope. You can't let her down.*

But it was so hard. I felt like I was losing my mind, along with my hope. I was still taking anti-depressants – even stronger ones now. But they didn't help. I could not have imagined feeling more desolate or despairing. On the anniversary, I sat by the window – *her* window – with a candle flickering on the sill beside me. Silently, I said my prayers.

'Please,' I pleaded. 'Please keep Charlene safe and warm and bring her home.

'Please carry her out of the darkness. Please.'

But soon after, the police came and Bob, Mum and I waited in the living room for the announcement we already knew was coming; they were scaling down their inquiry. It was no shock, but I was devastated all the same. She had been missing for almost a year, yet it felt like forever.

'We've been working very hard, we've interviewed hundreds upon hundreds of people,' explained our family liaison officer, 'But we have no further news for you, Karen. I am so sorry.'

The tears streamed down my cheeks and I felt Mum take my hand in hers. Bob swore and slammed out of the room.

'We'll keep it open, always. We'll never give up the search,' she added.

CHAPTER FOURTEEN

SWEET 16

I felt cheated and angry. To me, the longer Charlene was away, the worse it got. That day, 1st November 2003, was scorched onto my wounded and battered soul. From a mild annoyance that she was staying out late, it had fizzed up into a desperate worry, a screaming panic, a white-hot fear, that consumed every waking and sleeping moment of my life. Where was my daughter? Nobody knew. Nobody even seemed to care. Each milestone after Charlene's disappearance was a hurdle. I found myself dreading even more Mother's Days, birthdays and holidays; I didn't look forward to anything. Occasionally, Mum would arrange to take me back to Coventry for a few days, to stay with friends. I didn't really like going away – it was silly, but I felt that if I was in the house, Charlene was more likely to come home. If her bed was left empty, and her window was unmanned, she might never come.

'It's just for two days,' Mum persuaded me. 'Bob's in the house, and Becki and Emma are not far away. They'll let us know if anything happens.'

Charlene was on my mind, all the time. There was no escape, nor did I want one. As her 16th birthday approached, I viewed it with a growing sense of both panic and excitement. I couldn't begin to think how I could get through such an important day without her there and yet part of me felt that this might be the day she came home too. And so, whilst I dreaded her birthday, I couldn't wait for it either. I went off to Asda and asked them to make a birthday cake with her photo on the top.

'It's for my daughter,' I told them. 'She's going to be 16.'

By now, Charlene's face was well known in Blackpool. But the bakers were interested only in getting through their shift and doing their job. Nobody recognised her – or admitted they did. And I was grateful for that. I wasn't sure whether I might be seen as crazy, buying a cake for a child who wasn't there. But what else could I do? What kind of parent would ignore their child's birthday? On the day itself I laid out the cake with a fancy tablecloth. I had bought a 16th card and put some money inside. I blew up balloons and Bob hung a 'Happy 16th Birthday!' banner.

Emma and Becki came, and Robert was even allowed home for a short visit.

'Is she coming?' he asked me excitedly, as he ran in through the door.

He had made her a card himself and as he put it down on the table, my eyes swam with tears. I hesitated – I didn't know what to tell him, I didn't want to make him cry. That whole afternoon, I sat by the window until I could physically bear it no longer. Looking out onto the empty street, my heart leaping and plummeting with every new stranger who came into view, was torturous. I was crucifying myself. Worse still, my children were carrying the cross. Martin called round, now a young man himself, and he burst into tears when he saw Charlene's cake.

'I miss my Charley-Farley!' he sobbed. 'I wish she'd come home!'

'I know, Martin, I know,' I said, cradling his head in my arms.

Night came, but Charlene didn't arrive. Dejected and tear-stained, Emma, Becki and Robert all went off to their new homes. Mum went off to bed, and Bob took himself off out. And I was left alone, with my memories and my tears. The 'Happy Birthday' banner seemed to leer and gloat at me from the wall so I ripped it down and stuffed it in the bin. I blamed the stupid banner and the balloons; I blamed the police and the media for not listening. And I blamed Blackpool, too – the town we once loved had swallowed her whole and was refusing to give her back. Out of Charlene's bedroom window, through the darkness, I could see the twinkling lights of the North Pier and I was gripped by a fear so fierce it threatened to suffocate me.

Don't lose hope, Karen, I told myself firmly.

It was my mantra; I clung to it. What else did I have? And so the agony dragged on and I began to fear it would always be so.

CHAPTER FIFTEEN

A BREAKTHROUGH

One Friday morning, in March 2006, two officers from the Criminal Investigation Department (CID) knocked on our door.

'What is it?' I asked.

'We'd like to see you next Tuesday,' said one. 'Down at the station with the senior officer.'

My mouth went so dry, I could barely get the words out: 'What's happened?' I croaked. 'Have you found her? Have you found my Charlene?'

But the officer simply shook his head.

'We'll send a car on Tuesday,' he said. 'I'm sorry, that's all I can say.'

'Please,' I pleaded, 'is she alive? Just tell me that much.'

The tears streamed down my cheeks, but they refused to say another word. I was still standing on my doorstep, dumbstruck with the news, as the police car disappeared at the top of our street. Eventually, I heard Bob, shouting from the back room.

'What did they want?' he called.

'The police want to see us next week,' I replied. 'The top bloke, as well.'

I wasn't sure why, but there was an excitement, a lift in my voice. I went over and over the conversation in my mind. The officers had been professional, but friendly. They had offered to send a car for us. The senior officer, Paul Buschini, would be there. I had only met him once before. Surely then this had to be good news? If Charlene was dead, they would have told us there and then. No point in hiding the fact. Certainly, no reason for us to go to the police station. The only reason to visit the station would be if our daughter was there too. It was so obvious, so blindingly simple, that I started to laugh out loud like a drunk, amazed at my own stupidity.

'Of course!' I shouted out loud. 'Of course!'

The most likely scenario, I decided, was that they had found Charlene, kidnapped, held against her will, just as I had always known. That explained the four-day delay – she would need to be seen by specialist officers, interviewed and examined. It was vital they spoke to her first, got her account, whilst it was still fresh in her mind. I understood that. Now, as the glimmer of hope burned stronger, I could be patient. Magnanimous. Grateful. Oh, and how grateful. How had they found her? Maybe it was a tip-off from a member of the public. Perhaps it was part of a raid on a known gang, paedophiles or people traffickers. I had no idea about gangs and that sort of thing. But I had known for certain, all along, she was in the dark. I had sensed it, as a mother. Maybe the police had to keep quiet, until the arrests were made and the gang was caught. It all made sense to me now. My little girl would be traumatised, hurt, damaged. But alive. *Alive*. And that was all that mattered now. I could heal her, help her; love her back to health.

I closed my eyes, my pulse quickening with excitement, and imagined our reunion in the specialist crisis suite at the police station or wherever these things were held. Greedily, I replayed the scene again and again, gulping in the details of her face, her little hands, her black and gold jeans. Would she still have the same clothes? No matter, I would buy her more. A thousand pairs of jeans. Dozens of times, I fast-forwarded to the part where she fell into my arms and we sobbed together, and I held her like I'd never let her go again.

My Charlene was coming home!

I wanted to scream it from the top of the roof; to hand out leaflets on the pier. I wanted to call Darren Day and let him know too! Nothing else mattered. The washing machine could flood, the red gas bill could arrive … I

would laugh at it all and nothing would ever worry me
again. Because my daughter, my darling Charlene, was
coming home! That day – and the whole weekend –
stretched ahead endlessly. Mum and I went shopping, we
watched TV, we did our best to fill in the hours which
stretched ahead of us. Bob pottered around the house and
tinkered with his bike. But the minutes seemed to drag. I
couldn't wait to see my little girl again.

* * *

The car arrived, on Tuesday, as promised. Bob and I left
Mum at home and were driven to the station, sitting in
total silence on the back seat. As the moment drew nearer,
I was suddenly not so brave, not so confident. All at once,
time was racing, along with my heart; I felt sick.

Paul Buschini, head of the Major Investigation Unit,
was a small, neat man with a shiny bald head. He offered
out a hand.

'Can I get you a brew?' he asked.

That's good news, I told myself. *He's friendly.*

We were shown into a room, which looked like a
working office. There were computers, desks, papers piled
everywhere, and seats waiting for us, opposite Buschini.

I could wait no longer.

'Have you found her?' I blurted out. 'Please say it's
good news. *Please*.'

'There is a development.' He nodded.

The words seemed to roll so slowly out of his mouth, syllable by syllable. I couldn't stand the suspense. And then, they shot out, all in a rush, like vomit, and slapped me full in the face.

'I am so sorry. I have bad news: we believe Charlene has been murdered.'

It felt like an invisible hand was strangling my heart. With a scream, I dropped the boiling coffee into my lap. But I didn't even feel the pain; I didn't notice the mess. I heard a voice shrieking and then I realised it was mine. Buschini looked straight at me and said: 'I am 99.9 per cent certain that your daughter has been murdered, and the two suspects are being arrested as we speak.'

I was hysterical; I had thought there was good news waiting. Instead, I was falling further and further into a black pit of hopelessness. I could hear Bob gasping and swearing beside me, but he sounded as though he was a long way away, somehow. Like he was down a tunnel.

'Why wasn't I told?' I demanded. 'Why didn't I know? She's my daughter.'

'We're telling you now,' he said. 'We're making arrests.'

Arrests? And I realised suddenly the second part of what he was telling me.

'Who is it?' I yelled. 'Who did it?'

I was on my feet now, pacing the small room, hot and agitated. There were a million questions. *Did we know the suspects? Did they know us?* But the police couldn't tell us any more. We had to go home and wait, Buschini said. *Wait.* Like that wasn't what I'd been doing for the past two years.

'We'll go and speak to your daughters,' he added. 'We'll visit Robert, too, in Manchester. We will do everything we can to support you.'

Now, I noticed bitterly, they couldn't do enough for us. They were quietly efficient and kind. If only they had been like that from the start. But this new attentiveness was alarming too. They tiptoed around us, mopping up the spilt coffee, nodding sympathetically, speaking in hushed tones as though this was a funeral. As though we were *bereaved*.

My God, it hit me: *We are bereaved, our daughter is dead.*

The thought hadn't made it from one neuron to the next before I angrily chased it back again.

No, we are not bereaved, I told myself furiously. *Charlene is alive. What do the police know? Pull yourself together.*

All the way home, the two voices battled in my head. By the time we got there, specialist officers had already been to Emma and Becki's flat and brought them to us.

They sobbed, heartbroken.

'Mum, say it's not true,' Emma wept. '*Please.*'

But I had no words of relief for her pain. We were all reeling, spinning. Mum slumped on the couch, her head in her hands, sobbing. She was a strong, steely woman, but this had beaten her.

Within half an hour, there was a press pack on our doorstep. Shocked, I spotted reporters peering through the windows, tapping on the glass with their posh pens. One got so close, I could see his nasal hair as he peered into our living room, beckoning me over with a nauseating smile. It was the same window where I sat, every night, to look out for Charlene. *How dare he use her window, her altar?* I felt invaded, violated. For more than two years, nobody had listened, nobody had cared. I had pleaded with the police and the press to help me find my daughter. Only now, when they thought she was dead, were they taking an interest. It was a topsy-turvy world; a sick and salacious world – and I no longer wanted to be a part of it.

'Go away!' I yelled, indignant with rage. 'Get away from her window and leave us alone!'

But instead, they skulked back into their cars and waited on the street outside, watching our house as though there were fugitives inside. Normally, Bob would have been raging, marching up and down the street and frightening them all away. But this was not normal.

And Bob, catatonic in the corner of the living room, said nothing.

That same night, at 9pm, Mr Buschini knocked on our door.

'We've charged two men,' he told us. 'One with the murder of Charlene, one with helping to dispose of her body.'

My blood ran cold. Disposing of a body, perversely, sounded even worse than the murder itself. It was so cold. So final. So clinical.

'Are you sure?' I pleaded. 'Could there be a mistake?'

Part of me didn't want to listen, because I wouldn't – *couldn't* – believe that my daughter was dead. I wanted to clamp my hands over my ears and shut it all out.

Buschini told us that two men, Iyad Albattikhi and Mohammed Raveshi, were joint owners of a local take-away called Funny Boyz – just a few minutes' walk away from our home. I had expected, somehow, to recognise the names; to have some connection with the people who had destroyed our lives. But the names meant nothing to me. I had never, ever heard of them. Doubtless, I had walked past the takeaway many times. I had certainly looked out upon it, from Charlene's bedroom window, and seen the sickly neon haze below. The police told us they had searched the takeaway, and other premises, but had yet to find Charlene's body.

'Well, that's something,' I croaked, clutching on to whatever I could.

With no body, I still had hope. But it was barely a flicker. And that night, as I lay in Charlene's bed, I racked my brains and realised I had already forgotten the men's surnames. How could I? These men were accused of taking my daughter from me. But somehow, their names had disappeared from my mind.

'You'll have to prepare for a court case,' Buschini had told us. 'This is going to be very difficult.'

CHAPTER SIXTEEN

AN EMPTY SEAT

And Mr Buschini was right. As our lives unravelled further, in those weeks afterwards, Bob turned inwards and sank deeper into himself. He was unable to verbalise the revulsion and the outrage that surely coursed through his veins, as it did mine. But I could not remain silent. I wanted to reach out – to look for help – to tell the world. Desperate for more information, Mum and I walked round the local takeaways, blinking in the glare of the glitzy signs, gagging on the thick smells of cheap cooking fat and disinfectant. Pressing my face against the windows, condensation streaming down the glass, I let the tears flow.

'Where are you, Charlene?' I sobbed. 'Please come home.'

I knew we couldn't approach the two men and I wouldn't have known what to do if we did. A piece of me wanted to scream and tear them limb from limb. I was a peaceful woman, but I wished a biblical pain and suffering on them both. And yet a bigger part of me just wanted to run away from them, pretend it hadn't happened and believe my Charlene might still be coming home. The days passed in a horrible limbo; grey, hopeless and meaningless. The journalists left us alone after those first few, manic hours. I was robotic; processing each task mechanically. Bob hid behind the booze. I never missed a visit to see Robert, but his social workers openly admitted that his behaviour was as much of a problem now as ever. It was another worry to pile on top of all the others. I was so thankful for Emma and Becki popping in, or calling me up to talk about their lives.

'You girls keep me sane,' I told them.

Somewhat hollowly, they laughed. But it was true. And Mum, as always, was there for me; my light in the blackness. But she shone more feebly as the stress weighed heavier on her. Sometimes, I wondered if she would live long enough to see the court case. In July 2006, we were given a trial date, for May 2007. The date would mark three and half years since I had last seen my daughter. I wanted to face these men yet I was dreading it too. I needed the truth, but I didn't want confirmation that Charlene was dead. I didn't want people to give up on her, the search had to go on. In March of that same year, it was Charlene's 18th birthday. Now, more than ever, I needed her home. But it seemed less and less likely. The possibility that she was dead loomed huge and ugly, like a sea monster, in my dreams each night. I couldn't bear to go through the agony of the previous three birthdays, where we had sat and waited like lambs to the slaughter: anxious, accepting, beaten. I couldn't sit by the window again, not this year. Sometimes, I felt like smashing the glass and slitting my wrists with the shards. Yet neither could I let her birthday pass, if not with celebration, then at least with recognition.

'We have hope,' Mum told me with a weary smile. 'There's no body so we still have hope.'

I booked dinner at a restaurant on the promenade for our whole family. It was almost lovely, there was just one person missing. I had bought her a birthday card and put some money inside.

Just in case, I told myself, as I licked the envelope.

Afterwards, we went to Stanley Park, the town's biggest park and a place that Charlene had loved as a little girl. We released balloons, in her memory, and we held each other and cried. That night, back at home, I slipped her birthday card into a drawer, along with the others.

'It's here for you, Babby,' I whispered softly. 'And it always will be.'

CHAPTER SEVENTEEN

TRADED FOR A BAG OF CHIPS

A week before the trial began, two police officers arrived and took us to Preston Crown Court.

'We just want you to be familiar with the courts,' explained our liaison officer. 'There's nothing to worry about.'

It was the first time I'd ever been inside a courtroom. The hushed silence and the air of austerity was daunting. I felt suddenly rather scruffy and badly dressed; I couldn't even remember running a brush through my hair that morning. I was annoyed that I could even be thinking of my own hair on such a serious occasion, but at the same time I was wishing I had made a bit more of an effort. A clerk glanced at me disapprovingly, over her glasses, and I reddened, as though I had done something wrong myself. *Was she thinking the same thing about my hair?* This was a world away from my life and I didn't belong here. We were introduced to our barrister, Tim Holroyde. He swept in, robes flowing, wig jauntily sitting on his head, like a character out of a period drama. I half-expected him to draw an old-fashioned pistol from his belt and shoot the lot of us. He gave me the briefest of smiles.

'Are the family prepared for what they will hear in court?' he asked imperiously.

The officer shook her head.

'No,' she replied.

There was a ponderous silence. I had no idea what they were talking about; nobody thought to tell me and I certainly didn't have the confidence to speak up and ask. We were driven back home and I felt no more prepared for the court case than I would be for the electric chair. The trial was weighing heavily on my mind. There was the huge, overpowering fear of facing the two men. The dark dread of hearing what had happened to my darling daughter. But, incredibly, smaller, trivial concerns managed to wriggle their way in there too. I worried how I would be viewed and portrayed.

In the end, I decided to buy a new outfit. It was a decision I struggled with. I didn't want to spend money on new clothes, as if I was going to a party – it seemed ghoulish.

But I wanted to look smart, for Charlene. I wanted her to be proud of me, wherever she was. And I didn't want the barristers and the solicitors looking down their noses at me, thinking Charlene didn't matter so much because her mother didn't have a decent pair of shoes on.

Get some nice trousers, Mum, said a little voice in my head. *You always suit trousers.*

I could hear Charlene speaking as if she was right next to me, looking me up and down, hands on hips. Emma came shopping with me; she had such a good taste in clothes that I always relied on her judgement. There was a little shop in Blackpool that sold larger sizes and so we went in there.

'What's the occasion?' asked the shop assistant with a saccharine smile.

Emma and I both froze and said nothing. We settled on a brown trouser suit, with a patterned blouse and flat brown shoes. It was a nice enough outfit, but I wanted to burn it. I had such a pain across my chest that at times I thought I might be having a heart attack. I worried I might die before the trial even started. How much stress could any woman take? Only my love for Charlene, and my desire for the truth, kept me strong. Emma got herself a new outfit too, a white blouse, black skirt and black heels. Mum decided to wear a nice dress she'd worn just once before, on her birthday, and I suggested that Bob wore his best grey jacket, white shirt, and black trousers. But Becki didn't want to buy anything.

'I'll wear what I've got,' she insisted quietly. 'When the time comes.'

I was worried about them both, but especially Becki. I knew she'd be reliving that last day and blaming herself, all over again. It was as if we had all been dumped back on 1st November 2003 and we had to suffer it all once more. The night before I was due to give evidence, I didn't sleep one bit. But I felt wired; wide awake, as if I could run a marathon. Emma tapped on the door at 7am: she had come to help me get ready and do my hair.

'Up or down?' she asked, ready with the hairbrush.

I shrugged anxiously. Was it not unseemly to be deliberating over my hairstyle for my daughter's murder trial? And yet again, it was these little things that consumed me.

'Down,' I said eventually. 'Less fuss.'

'Put a bit of make-up on,' Emma persuaded me. 'Everyone will be looking at you, Mum. You need to look smart.'

I never wore make-up – it made me feel uncomfortable and showy, like I was painting on a new face. And maybe that was just how it was. This was the third day of the trial. I hadn't been allowed to go so far, because I was a witness. Those first three days, the case against the two men had been outlined. It was the prosecution's belief that Charlene had been murdered by Iyad Albattikhi, a 29-year-old Jordanian man, the owner of 'Funny Boyz' fast-food takeaway in Blackpool. Mohammed Raveshi, Albattikhi's 50-year-old Iranian business partner, was accused of disposing of her body. The jury was told that there were covert tape recordings of the two men, which would prove the case against them. I had no idea, beyond this, what to expect.

'We can't give you any more information, Karen, because we don't want to compromise the case,' our liaison officer had explained.

I understood that. But I felt so insignificant, so shut out. This was my daughter's murder trial and I was no more than a spectator, a forgotten extra. And it hurt. I hadn't been given any advice from the CPS or my liaison officers, I didn't know what to prepare for, but today, I was due to give evidence. I had to be ready.

The car arrived, as planned, to take Bob, Mum and me to court. Emma and Becki were travelling separately. The driver played Kaiser Chiefs, at full volume, all the way to Preston Crown Court.

'Ruby, Ruby, Ruby, Ruby!' screamed the radio.

The noise was tinny, scraping against my brain. But it didn't even occur to me to ask the driver to turn it down; there was such chaos inside my head. The music just added to my confusion. I hadn't managed any breakfast and I started to feel nauseous and light-headed. Outside the court, there was a crush of photographers, jostling for a picture – of us, I realised. *Good job I had my new outfit*, I told myself. *Money well spent*. Such frivolity was shocking. Inappropriate. But that was just the sort of thing Charlene would have said too; she saw the joke in everything. I had to swallow hard and keep the tears at bay.

Not now, Karen, I thought firmly. *Don't let her down. Not now*.

I wasn't allowed into court, because I had to give my evidence later. But Mum and the girls went in, whilst I waited in one of the witness rooms upstairs. The manager of Robert's care home, a man called Dave Smith, brought Robert in too.

'We thought it best that he didn't feel left out,' explained Dave. 'He deserves to know what's going on.'

I nodded gratefully – he was very thoughtful. I was allowed to give Robert a quick hug before he went to join the others. The liaison officers were very kind too; they kept me busy with a constant supply of coffee and tea. But I just wanted to be in court; I wanted to be with my family. Charlene was my daughter and to me it seemed absurd that I was banned from the room. Then, we got a message that the court had finished early for the day and I wasn't needed yet, after all, so I was allowed to go downstairs. As I caught sight of Mum's face as she walked down the corridor, I felt a chill run through me.

'What is it?' I gasped. 'What's happened?'

Mum looked shell-shocked. Emma, a yellowy white, dashed straight into the toilets and I could hear her retching.

'Prepare yourself,' Mum whispered. 'They chopped her up. They minced her, they sold her …'

Robert came running towards me and collapsed in my arms.

'Mummy!' he sobbed.

Even Dave seemed close to tears.

'I feel for you, Mrs Downes,' he said quietly. 'You shouldn't have to go through that. I won't bring Robert back tomorrow, if you don't mind.'

I did my best to comfort Robert before we had to say goodbye – I didn't want him to have to leave, but Emma needed me too. My mind was reeling. I didn't know who to hug first. It felt like Rome was burning all around me and I had just a measly glass of water to fight the fire. Mum and Bob didn't speak in the car. Bob looked wounded, shell-shocked. He was muttering under his breath.

'I don't want you to go in there,' was all Mum said to me. 'I don't want you to hear it.'

I knew she wasn't allowed to discuss the case with me, because I was a prosecution witness. In a way, I felt deflated. It was such an anti-climax. I had built myself up for this, only to be sent home. And it made the wait, and the stress, hang heavier and heavier on me. Again that night, I dozed only in short, sharp stretches. I felt as if even my sleep was frenzied and fraught with worry. Mum's words had added another layer of worry to the panic and dread I was already feeling. I tried not to dwell on them. The next morning, I went through it all again – the hair, the make-up – the same outfit with a new blouse – but the whole routine made me want to throw up.

'Prepare yourself,' Mum told me tearfully.

At the door to the court, I felt like running. Turning and running as far as my new flat shoes would carry me. But I was Charlene's mother. She had just one mother – just one hope. And this was my time to be strong. This time, I was shown to the witness stand. A sea of faces swam before me. I shook, uncontrollably, as I was handed the Bible to swear an oath. My barrister came first.

'I understand you're nervous,' he said, with a smile. 'Please don't be.'

He asked me when Charlene's birthday was. He asked when I had last seen her. And also, he said: 'Were you close to your daughter?'

At these words, a tremendous tsunami of love and emotion swelled my chest. I saw Charlene's little face, smiling, in my mind and I replied: 'Yes, very close. I loved her very much. And I still do.'

Giving evidence, I was firm, sure; brave. The defendants didn't even look my way, as if I was an inconsequence to them.

Show them, Karen, I steeled myself. *Show them and everyone else.*

Next, a defence barrister questioned me.

'Was Charlene a happy child?' he asked.

I insisted that she was. But I felt I was over-insisting, in the way that you can over-state the truth until it looks as though you're lying. I was getting flustered.

He asked why I had waited 24 hours before calling the police after she vanished.

'That's not correct,' I replied, trying hard to hide the resentment in my tone. 'I called the police and they told me I had to wait 24 hours – I had no choice.'

And that was it: my evidence was done.

'Please can I join my family in the gallery here?' I asked nervously.

'Of course you may,' the judge replied.

Charlene's friends gave evidence next. But I didn't know all of them and that surprised me. There were girls I had never even seen before, who claimed to know Charlene well. They seemed older too; more street-wise than my little girl. Charlene's closest friend, Martin, wasn't even called to the trial.

How do they know her? I wondered.

I looked at Emma and Becki – they seemed just as confused as I was. And I was taken aback by some of the barrister's questions for the girls. I didn't understand the relevance. They were asked if they knew any of the men who worked in the takeaways. And if they'd ever had free food or cigarettes offered to them.

What does that have to do with my daughter's death? I wondered.

Then the prosecution barrister turned to the jury, paused dramatically, and said that Charlene was one of a number of young girls who visited an alleyway in Blackpool to have sex with older men in the takeaways.

No, I gasped to myself, *that can't be true!*

But one of the girls, on the witness stand, then confirmed she had been offered food from local takeaway workers in return for sexual favours. I stared in disbelief.

'A bag of chips for a blow-job,' said another girl.

My stomach turned. Every girl questioned confirmed that Charlene knew the defendants. She had been given free chips; it wasn't difficult to work out the next piece of the puzzle. I felt sick inside. That couldn't be right, not my daughter. But how could all those girls be wrong? Their words turned over and over in my mind.

I had opened a door and I wanted to shut it again.

CHAPTER EIGHTEEN

MEDIA FEEDING FRENZY

Slowly, painfully, the trial moved on, and each morning I went through the same routine. I felt something of a sick fraud. Each day, I put on a smart outfit and my make-up, as if I was off to a party. Each night, I came home feeling as though I'd had my heart ripped out. I was learning more and more about Charlene, sitting in that courtroom each day as the trial went on.

Just over a week into the trial, Mr Holroyde, QC, said: 'A witness heard Albattikhi and others talking about Charlene. They were talking about sex with white girls and there was mention of having sex with Charlene.

'Albattikhi laughed and said she was kinky and she was very small – the plainest possible indication that he was lying to the police when he said he did not know her. He and others present then laughingly said that Charlene had gone into the kebabs.'

He paused and then, in slow-motion horror, described how the prosecution believed that my daughter – my 14-year-old daughter – had been chopped up, minced and fed to unsuspecting customers in kebabs. Her bones, he said, had been ground down into tile grouting. I found that I was suddenly ice-cold, shaking. It was so disgustingly far-fetched, so utterly inhumane. I had come here for the truth, for justice, for a shred of comfort even, for my family, but the Charlene they described, groomed by Asian takeaway workers, swapping sex for chips, then murdered and minced was not one I recognised at all. I wanted to stand up in court and scream. They didn't know her, none of them did. There was no mention of Charlene, the little girl who sang along to Darren Day and still held her mum's hand. Realising I was going to be sick, I dashed from the court, with Mum close behind me. I slumped over the toilet bowl, on my knees, the tears falling fast.

'I'm going home,' I groaned. 'I can't take any more.'

'You can't leave now,' Mum said gently. 'Come on.'

But I couldn't carry on; I had thrown up all over myself. That afternoon, my mind buzzed with fresh turmoil. How could I not have known what was happening? Why couldn't I have saved her? My poor little girl had suffered.

She must have been so frightened. I couldn't allow myself to think about what had happened to her body; I knew I would have broken completely. I had no words. Mum was ashen-faced when she arrived home later on. I could see her ageing, visibly, as each day of the trial passed. And today, she looked as though the life had been knocked out of her completely.

'What do you think about what they said in court?' I asked her. 'About the Asian grooming gangs, the child sex rings?'

Mum shuddered.

'They never had those in my day, Karen,' she replied. 'I've never heard of anything like it. I can't believe our Charlene was caught up in all that.'

Neither could I. And yet the evidence was there. What had I missed? I thought back to the days she'd played truant from school. Was she being abused at the take-aways when she should have been sitting in class? Had these men bought her the cigarettes when I'd caught her smoking? I remembered I had grilled her about the cigarettes; I had been so disgusted that she was smoking. Little did I know this was just the tip of a very murky pool.

'They're not cheap, Charlene,' I had said angrily. 'Who bought cigarettes for you?'

But she had shrugged and giggled and skirted around the subject.

'My friends give me cigarettes,' she replied. 'My school friends.'

I had threatened to call her friends' parents and thrash it out with them but Charlene was so alarmed that I had backed down.

'Please don't, Mum,' she begged. 'My friends will never speak to me again if you do that. I'll stop smoking, I promise. I really do.'

There had a been brief period when she'd been bullied on the school bus too. I remembered it now. Nothing major; a few girls calling her names and upsetting her. It tugged at my heartstrings when she came home in tears.

'They hate me,' she sobbed. 'I daren't get on the bus tomorrow, please don't make me.'

As a kid, I'd been bullied myself. 'We'll sort it out,' I promised.

But before I got the chance to call her school and tell Charlene's teacher, Becki had marched onto the school bus the following morning and warned the bullies to leave her alone.

'They won't bother you again,' she had told Charlene.

And Charlene had smiled that sort of safe, contented smile that only children with older siblings to look after them will understand. And so, the bullying had been nipped in the bud almost before it had even started. I didn't see how that could have driven Charlene off the rails and into the clutches of a grooming gang, though. She'd started going out in the evenings and staying out later too. But it wasn't as if she went missing for days on end. I had thought she was out with her pals, on the pier or walking along the promenade. At 14, I thought they were buying milkshakes, discussing homework, giggling about boys. Doing the sort of things every normal teenager does. I could not have dreamt they were being so horribly and blatantly exploited. There had been one occasion, though, when Charlene came in from school and she had looked so pleased with herself that I'd asked why.

'I've got £70!' She grinned, waving a few £10 notes at me. 'All for me!'

I stared.

'Where on earth have you got £70 from?' I asked. 'Let me see, let me count it.'

Charlene backed away, sensing I was going to take it off her.

'It's mine, I can keep it,' she said defensively. 'I got it off a friend at school.'

'No way!' I said flatly. 'You wouldn't get £70 from a friend. And if you did, you'd have to give it straight back.'

Although I pressed and pressed her, she refused to tell me the friend's name. I knew she was lying; I wasn't even sure that she actually had £70. Perhaps that was a lie too. Even so, I'd seen some money in her hand and it was enough to worry me. I asked Mum to speak to her – she was much closer to Charlene than I was at that point – but even she couldn't get the truth from her.

'I tried talking to her, in bed last night,' Mum told me. 'But she just clammed up. I think she's hiding something, but I don't know what.'

It was a mystery.

'I think you're making a fuss about nothing,' Bob said eventually. 'She's winding you up.'

But it played on my mind. I knew Charlene was lying to me. And I never did get to the bottom of where the money had come from. Eventually, that mini-crisis was usurped by the next, as is the way in a busy family. But now the jigsaw seemed to slot together with a sickening precision. Was it dirty money? Money for sex? I shivered; I just couldn't make sense of it all. A maelstrom of emotions whirled around inside my brain. And the warped idea that Charlene had been served up, in kebabs, was as mind-boggling as it was evil. I had walked the streets, night after night, handing out the 'Missing' leaflets to holidaymakers, who were enjoying kebabs and burgers as they strolled past. Could it really be true? Had they been taking my leaflets and potentially eating my daughter? I felt myself taking a deep breath and I said, out loud: *Stop it now, Karen. Don't think about this.*

I had the rest of the trial to get through. Somehow I had to cope and I had to stay sane. I had to wear my best clothes, slick on my lipstick and sit in court like a half-deranged robot. And I knew that torturing myself with suggestions and allegations would have tipped me right over the edge. And so, I tried to block it out as best I could. But the next day, the sordid details of my daughter's horrific death were plastered all over the newspapers, the same newspapers who had refused to publish appeals when Charlene had first vanished. Now, they couldn't get enough of her. The articles described her as sleeping around, trading food and cigarettes for sex. She was 14 years old – a child.

Mum put her arms around me. But nothing could comfort me.

'They're making out like she was some sort of prostitute,' I wailed.

It felt as if they were blaming her and yet she was the victim.

'Animals,' I sobbed, 'the lot of them!'

CHAPTER NINETEEN
SHOCK LETTER

I thought I had hit rock bottom, but the trial moved on and there were more bombshells to come. It was claimed that Charlene had made 13 visits to a walk-in sexual health clinic during the two-year period before she vanished. Appalled, I was sure there had to be some mistake, but it was apparently all recorded by health professionals. I'd had absolutely no idea; I would have sworn blind that she didn't even know what a sexual health clinic was. As far as I knew, she had made two visits to the GP in the months before she vanished and my mum had gone with her on both occasions. One was to treat a suspected water infection and the other was because Charlene was getting bad headaches, around the time of her periods, and I wanted to get her checked out. I knew, looking back, that water infections could be caused by sex. But at the time, I didn't even think of it. Why would I? The idea was absurd.

'The GP says it's nothing to worry about,' Mum had told me later. 'But he says if the headaches don't ease off, we ought to see an optician. She may need glasses.'

Charlene had groaned and shook her head. And the headaches had cleared up, it was that simple. The idea that she had been making secret visits to a sexual health clinic was so ridiculous, it was almost laughable. One thing was for sure, she certainly hadn't gone there alone or of her own accord – she just wouldn't have known about such places. Somebody had organised it for her – but who? I was angry, too, that I hadn't been informed of her appointments there. Surely the staff could see she was only 14? Charlene was not one of those teenagers who, dolled up to the eyeballs, looks ten years older – she looked just like the little girl she was. If the staff at the clinic couldn't tell me, they should have told the police or social services. I knew there were confidentiality rules, designed to protect vulnerable clients. But it seemed to me that this had backfired. Nobody had been looking out for her at all. So why? I had so many questions.

But now the prosecution barrister was talking about an anonymous letter – a poison-pen letter – found in Charlene's bedroom, after our home was searched in November 2003, that first week Charlene had gone missing. Mum raised her eyebrows at me and I shrugged helplessly. Again, I had no idea what he was talking about, but as he began to read out the contents of the letter, my blood ran cold.

'I've been watching you, you dirty little bitch. I don't like girls who go with Pakis, they use you like a piece of shit. You should be in a box underground, you dirty cow. Get out of Blackpool, because I'm ready to put you below, still alive. You have been warned.'

The barrister stopped speaking and I thought my heart was going to stop too. I was revulsed, yet completely mystified too. The police had never mentioned the letter to me. This was something else I knew nothing about. I was starting to think this whole trial was some sort of sick conspiracy. I wanted to see it – check the handwriting, look at the type of paper. Who was writing letters like that to my daughter? I felt it was my place – my right, as her mother – to march up to the judge and demand to see it. I was bristling with anger and adrenaline. Anger too, at myself, as her mother: my little girl had been stuck in such a terrible mess, she was caught in such a frightening trap, and I hadn't even known about it. At the break, I ran breathlessly to find our liaison officer and asked for a copy of the letter.

'I'm afraid it's evidence,' she said. 'You can't see it now.'

I felt a scream rising up in my throat; I fled the court, sobbing. And as I left, I caught sight of one of the defendants, smirking from behind a glass screen. I wasn't sure how much more I could take, but there was no question of me giving in. I returned again and again, day after day, like a human sacrifice. Bob, Mum, and the girls came too, and though it was a support, it worried me that my daughters were being exposed to such horror. There was mention of the burial place for Charlene's body. I shuddered and my mind went back instantly to the psychic, who had said Charlene was submerged in water. She had described 'the burial place' to me in detail, as a marshy area. Could she have been right? But despite searches, said the barrister, there had been no trace of my daughter's body.

There were more witnesses, more claims. I had never met any of them or heard their stories before. So many of these people, slithering in and out of Charlene's life and death, were strangers to me. Their evidence was contradictory and stomach-churning. The dark, slimy underbelly of Blackpool was laid bare: the tawdry, seedy takeaways, the infamous 'Paki Alley', where white girls were supposedly groomed for sex. I had never even heard of it until now. But in court, it was described like some sort of thriving small business. I felt as though I'd been living in some sort of bubble; a murky, stomach-churning world of child sex abuse was hiding in plain sight, behind the bright lights and the tourist trade. Blackpool was a town famous for hen dos, stag parties and family holidays. And now child sex abuse. How had they ensnared my daughter, without me even realising? How had I been so blinkered? But looking back, I could see, with the tortuous wisdom of hindsight, that Charlene might indeed have been a soft target. Unlike her sisters, she was easily led and impressionable. When Becki moved schools, Charlene wanted to follow. She even managed to get herself expelled from school, to be with the big sister she idolised. And when Emma and Becki went out, Charlene was never far behind, tagging along faithfully, her eyes bright. And, of course, that was all well and good when the influences were positive, but Charlene had started smoking, playing truant. She had been staying out late with friends I didn't know. She didn't have Emma's maturity, or Becki's confidence. She didn't know how to say no.

Not yet.

Had they weighed up her quiet, giggly, girly nature and picked her out, as a hovering hawk picks out a baby mouse below? Was that how it worked? I felt certain that nobody would ever 'groom' Emma or Becki – Emma would give them a mouthful and Becki would likely give them a kick between the legs. But Charlene was sweet and vulnerable and so eager to please. Had those qualities I had always loved in her been her downfall? This was a tangled, sordid mess of lies upon lies. And through it all, Charlene seemed to be drifting further and further away.

One morning, on my way into court, I caught sight of a newsstand, with a headline that made me clench my jaw: 'Missing Madeleine: Parents' Heartache'.

'That's another missing child,' Mum said to me. 'I saw it on TV.'

My heart went out to her parents. But right now, I could think of nothing else but my own daughter.

* * *

Three tortuous months on, the closing speeches were done. My little girl's memory, her reputation, her character, had been dragged out and picked apart. She wasn't there to speak up for herself; I wasn't allowed to speak for her. These people knew, or claimed they knew, that Charlene had been a victim of a child sex gang. They knew that her body, her sweet smile, her chubby little hands, her shining eyes, had been shoved through a mincing machine. Bones snapped, skin torn, mind and soul ripped apart. Quite literally, she was little more – or little less – than a piece of meat. None of them had heard how beautifully she had sung 'Silent Night'. They hadn't seen her on a trolley dash around Morrisons; they didn't see the way her eyelashes rested on her baby-smooth cheeks when she slept.

As the jury retired, I was exhausted to the point of collapse. The two defendants had maintained their innocence throughout and claimed they did not even know

Charlene. But I felt sure, after everything we had heard, there would be a guilty verdict at the end of all this. Justice would be some small comfort. But the jury was out, day after day, without resolution. We waited, in limbo – it was like being stuck in purgatory. And, as time went on, and hell's heat burned nearer, I began to worry.

On the tenth day, the jury members finally came back and we took our places in the courtroom. My nerves jangled noisily as silence fell around us. The foreman stood up. My heart was thumping so hard, it felt like it would explode.

'We are unable to reach a verdict,' he announced.

There was an audible gasp around the court. Bob jumped up and began shouting and swearing. He had to be restrained by five or six security guards, who dragged him outside, his face pulsing with red rage, to calm down. I sat silent, suddenly smaller, lesser, as if someone had drained the last drop of blood from me. The jury was dismissed, the barristers and solicitors began to gather their papers and made arrangements to meet up over a glass of Chardonnay later that evening.

It was over.

'What happens now?' I asked quietly.

Dimly, I was aware of the two defendants chatting in the background, making plans for the future. Meanwhile, we had to pick up the shattered fragments of our lives and carry on. Outside the court, a pack of photographers swarmed towards us, zapping us with flash bulbs.

'How do you feel, Mrs Downes?' shouted a reporter.

I opened my mouth but the words didn't come. Back at home, we sat in stunned silence. Charlene had been ruined. Destroyed. And there was no justice for our family.

CHAPTER TWENTY
PICKING UP THE PIECES

After the trial, life seemed to move very slowly. I felt as though I was wading through cold and lumpy custard. Everything was so difficult. Bob and I barely spoke; the trial hadn't brought us closer together. The judge had praised us, as a family, for the way we had held ourselves during the trial. But in truth, what sort of 'family' did we have left? All too predictably, Bob had had to have his little outburst at the jury and ruin the judge's commendation of us as a unit.

'Don't you think I felt like screaming and shouting too, Bob?' I asked heatedly. 'We all did, but we behaved ourselves. We did it for Charlene.'

Bob was losing his temper, I was keeping the peace and yet, it was nothing like normal at all. Our problems, old problems – the nuisance neighbours, the struggle to make ends meet, even my silly fling – all seemed quite laughable now. We had come to Blackpool for a better life, but we had ended up straight in the lions' den.

Sitting at home, day after day, I stared at the TV: it was like white noise.

'There's that poor Madeleine girl again,' Mum remarked.

The disappearance of three-year-old Madeleine McCann was the top story on the *BBC 10 O'Clock News*.

'She's been on the news nearly every night for months,' Mum told me. 'You've missed it all, Karen. You've been in your own little world.'

I felt a rush of sympathy for her parents, but I was puzzled too: why had the media followed Madeleine's story and not Charlene's? It seemed like the whole world and his wife was looking for Gerry and Kate McCann's little girl, but nobody had looked for my daughter. I couldn't even get the local paper to run an appeal.

'Her parents have got money,' Bob observed drily. 'They've got people behind them, that's what it is.' I had to agree with him. Madeleine McCann's parents were educated, middle class, influential and respectable; they were everything I wasn't. Charlene had been a diffi-cult, wayward teen, but did that mean she mattered less? Madeleine's face was on every news channel, every magazine cover, every newspaper. And I couldn't help feeling resentful. Why was her life worth more than

Charlene's? One afternoon, only days after the end of the trial, I picked up a local paper and the headline sent a chill through my bones.

'Not another girl,' I groaned. 'Oh, no!'

Paige Chivers, a 15-year-old local girl, was missing from home.

We didn't know the girl, although she didn't live far from us, but I felt for her family. And it turned out that Emma knew Paige's younger brother, Jack. They were the same age and had knocked about in the same group of friends for a while.

'Her poor family,' I shuddered. 'I wouldn't wish it on anyone.'

I knew exactly what they were going through; I followed news reports of her case obsessively, hoping and praying she might come home. But she didn't. It brought back into sharp focus those days following Charlene's disappearance. I remembered how in court the barristers had claimed there were grooming gangs targeting dozens of young girls. It had seemed outlandish and I hadn't wanted to believe it. Now, I was not so sure. There were people with blood on their hands after Charlene's trial – they had barely had time to scrub them clean and now another young girl was missing. Another victim was crying out for help. I bought a newspaper each day, following her case – and wondering, too, if it might bring any news of

Charlene. The police said they could not rule out a link to Charlene's disappearance, nor could they find one.

Like Charlene, Paige had never left Blackpool alone before and she didn't own a passport when she disappeared. And just as with Charlene, detectives said they had questioned 3,000 people about her disappearance but were still none the wiser about where she had ended up. In 2014, Lancashire Police offered a £30,000 reward, promising to pay out to anyone who could help them find Paige's killer or her body.

What about my Charlene? I thought angrily.

It gnawed away at me. Didn't she matter? The following year, in February 2008, nine-year-old Shannon Matthews went missing in Yorkshire. Her disappearance hit the headlines, and again it was a mystery to me. It wasn't that I didn't want publicity for Madeleine McCann or Shannon Matthews. Sure, I did. I knew exactly how it felt to have a child go missing – I was part of that exclusive club no parent ever wants to join. But I wondered why had Charlene been ignored and discarded like the chip wrappers that blew down the same pier she had vanished from.

Maybe, with the Shannon Matthews case, the police had learned their lesson from Charlene's disappearance. At the start of 2005, a little over a year after Charlene's disappearance, they had launched the Awaken Project. This was a scheme jointly run by Blackpool Council and

Lancashire Police. Its aim was to safeguard vulnerable children and young people who were being sexually exploited, and also to identify, target and prosecute associated offenders. It was later credited with preventing more young girls from becoming victims of child sexual exploitation in Blackpool. But I didn't want my daughter to become a name on a training programme, a finger-wagging blueprint of how not to do things, I just wanted her home.

CHAPTER TWENTY-ONE
STABBED IN THE BACK

I wanted my son home too. Every two weeks, I would visit Robert, usually with Mum. Bob came with us occasionally, and so did the girls. But it wasn't easy, for Robert was filled with a new anger now – at the courts, at the justice system, at the press. More than ever, he was taunted by the other lads in the children's home too.

'Did your sister taste good in that kebab?' they laughed. 'Yum, yum!'

Robert reacted in the only way he now knew how: with violence. He was in and out of trouble with the police and the youth courts. He was put on various behaviour programmes. But nothing really seemed to touch him, to have an impact. Occasionally, he was allowed to come home for a visit, but only under supervision. One day, just before Christmas 2007, he was allowed a visit home, but the social worker came with him and never left his side.

'It's for his own safety,' he explained.

But I hated it. Having strangers in the house, watching our every move, writing reports about us, was horrible. Sometimes, I felt Robert was even further away from me than Charlene. As a mother, I felt like a first-class failure. And each big event – a family birthday, a wedding or a christening – just rubbed salt into my smarting wounds. Whilst everyone else celebrated, I was more miserable than ever. These 'special' days served only to remind me that my daughter was gone, and I hated them. I was becoming increasingly resentful and twisted and I didn't even like who I was any more.

The police called early in the New Year of 2008 to tell us that the retrial was scheduled to take place in April. Again, a few weeks before, we were taken to look around the courtroom; it was a different room this time, but the smell and the atmosphere were the same. But this time, I wasn't overly anxious or subservient – I was done with that. My dose of British Justice had left me defiant and contemptuous, I had little faith left. This time there would be no new outfit, no shiny shoes for me.

One week before the trial was due to start, we were asked to attend the police station, to meet with our new barrister and someone from the Crown Prosecution Service

(CPS). Our liaison officers would be there too. As was the routine now, a car came to collect Bob, Mum and me. And as was the routine, I had no idea what to expect. We took our seats in a small interview room. There was a horrible silence and I sensed something major was about to happen.

'We've brought you here today because we're dropping the case,' said the woman from the CPS. 'Evidential difficulties. I'm so sorry, no retrial.'

On hearing this, I exploded. I didn't even feel it, it just happened – it came from nowhere. I found myself shaking with white-hot fury.

'You can't!' I snapped. 'You *can't*!'

'We have already made the decision,' she replied. 'And I am sorry.'

But her apology only served to anger me further. And then the barrister said something which left me reeling.

'Would you like to go to court to see the defendants formally discharged?' he asked.

What kind of monster would ask a mother that? I couldn't believe what I was hearing. Did they think I had no feelings – no sensitivities – at all? Slowly, deliberately, I closed my eyes: the calm before the storm.

'Get me home,' I said quietly.

I was suddenly so cold and controlled that I was frightening myself. And I was about to lose it so spectacularly that nobody in that room would ever forget my rage.

'Get me home,' I repeated.

I stood up, pushed the table, and erupted again. I felt Mum steering me firmly out of the room and into the fresh air. My screams echoed all the way down the street.

'Calm down, Karen. You're out of your mind,' she said.

And she was right, I was. I wasn't aware of the journey home or what I did when I got there. Apoplectic, I grabbed a pen and paper and scrawled my thoughts into a letter.

'You had better hope I never come across you again,' I wrote furiously. 'Thanks to you, my daughter will never have justice. Look over your shoulder because if I ever see you, I will kill you.'

Mum peered over my shoulder and gasped.

'You can't send that!' she shrieked. 'Karen! What on earth are you thinking?'

I snarled and addressed the letter to the woman at the CPS.

'I will do what I want,' I spat.

I knew it was wrong. *Good*, I thought. *I would probably be arrested. Good again. I'd have a criminal record. I might go to jail. I was going mad. Good. All Good!* I licked a stamp and slapped it on the envelope. Posting it, I felt not a shred of regret. I marched back home, anger surging through me, too riled to even think about sleep. The following morning, I waited at the dining table, drumming my fingers, itching for a row with Bob.

'What?' he mumbled, shuffling in for his breakfast. 'What are you looking at me like that for?'

I growled and marched out again – I found I couldn't sit still or concentrate on anything at all. Late in the day, one of the officers on the case knocked on the door. I knew, immediately, what he wanted.

'Yes, it was me,' I snapped. 'All me.'

'I know why you sent it,' he said. 'But you have to stop. You can't send threats like that.'

I wasn't arrested or even charged; the officer was very kind. But I didn't want kindness or understanding – I was way past caring what happened to me. I didn't write any more letters, but the anger was there, bubbling away like a poison under my skin. For so long I had been 'passive Karen', keeping my grief to myself, suffering alone, crying silently into the darkness. I had complied with everything, agreed with everyone. And now, with my daughter cut adrift, that was going to change.

I was in a state I had never experienced before. I'd never taken drugs, but I imagined this was a similar feeling. Had my body been taken over, or had I left it behind – was this an out-of-body experience? I couldn't even make it through to the end of that thought to reach a conclusion. All logic, all reason, had gone. Furious, I was a pressure cooker of resentment and hurt, waiting to boil over. I went out to the supermarket in a state of rage and steamrollered my way past all the other shoppers, almost willing someone to confront me – to complain about me. I was desperate to argue, to fight. But everyone stood back. I was almost untouchable – and that just annoyed me even more.

'What's the matter with them all?' I seethed.

I walked home, fists clenched, teeth clamped together so tightly that my jaw ached. That evening, as I peeled potatoes, my outrage grew and grew. I couldn't have swallowed anything myself, my throat felt tight and dry. And yet I found myself peeling potatoes. I felt almost delirious with temper. That night, I sobbed for hours in Charlene's room. My thoughts and dreams were infected with the pearls of poison I'd heard at the trial. They were driving me mad; *I* was driving myself mad.

'Where is the justice?' I shouted. 'Why is there no retrial? Why have they dropped the case? What about my daughter?'

At 6am, three days after the trial had been abandoned, I was shouting and sobbing at an imaginary judge and jury.

'If I could get my hands on the woman at the CPS,' I seethed. 'If I could see that barrister. If I could ...'

Then, I heard grumbling and Bob appeared in his pyjamas.

'I am trying to sleep,' he implored. 'You're off your head, Karen.'

'I am not!' I yelled. 'I want justice! I won't stop!'

I sobbed and wailed, wringing my hands, wandering from room to room. A mind and body displaced. Demented.

'Leave me alone,' I pleaded. 'I don't want you here.'

'I will not!' Bob rapped. 'I want you to shut up.'

He seemed almost exasperated by my tears, annoyed that I was upset. I couldn't comprehend that he just wanted to go back to bed and sleep, as if nothing had happened.

'You should want justice too!' I yelled accusingly. 'You're her father!'

Bob growled and I saw his mouth twitch. His eyes bulged like an angry toad as he leaned over me and the stench of stale beer made me gag.

'I am glad she's dead,' he bawled. 'I hope you never find her!'

I stared at him, my eyes wild, my heart thumping against my chest. I couldn't breathe, I couldn't see properly. And in that moment, I hated him – I wanted him dead. I ran into the kitchen and on the draining board I spotted the same vegetable knife I had used to scrape the potatoes the previous evening. And all in a rush, in my mind's eye, I saw Bob with a bag of potatoes, held high above his head, as the poor social worker ran from the house and Robert's fate was sealed. I saw him throw the potatoes, I saw the glint of the potato knife. In the next moment, the knife was in my hand and I was running back into the living room.

'You bastard!' I screamed, lunging towards him. 'I'm going to kill you!'

'Stop it, you stupid bitch!' Bob snarled.

He grabbed my hand and twisted my wrist to try and get the knife. But the adrenaline was coursing through me. I managed to wriggle free. He ran, and I followed. I stabbed him, as hard as I could, in the back, just below the shoulder. Blood spurted everywhere: down the handle of the knife, over my hands, onto the floor. I fell to my knees, exhausted. Crushed. He turned to me, slow and stupid with shock.

'You stupid bitch,' he repeated. 'You stabbed me!'

I was aware of Mum at my side, her arms encircled around me, gently taking the knife and leading me to the sofa.

'This has to stop,' she said. 'Stop it now, Karen.'

'I wanted to kill him,' I told her. 'I still do.'

I had never been one to tell lies and I wasn't about to start now. Bob slammed out of the house; I didn't care whether I ever saw him again. We cleaned up the blood, but I felt no regret. Mum made us a cup of tea.

'It's all OK now,' she said calmly. 'It's over.'

As the adrenaline seeped out of me, I felt suddenly so worn out that I could barely keep my eyes open.

'I think I'll go and lie down,' I said wearily.

But just then, there was a tap at the door and I knew it had to be the police. I opened it and invited the officers inside. Mum jumped up from her chair, livid.

'How could he?' she seethed. 'After all you've been through, after what he said to you ...'

'It's OK, Mum,' I said patiently. 'He has every right to report it.'

I went quietly to the police station. It was the same station where I'd been earlier that week, to hear that the trial and my daughter were being abandoned by the people who should have been on her side. I shook as I went into the interview room.

'We understand you're under a lot of stress,' said the officer. 'But Bob has made a complaint and so we do need to speak with you.'

I didn't care about being in trouble. Despite all the blood, the police said it had been a minor flesh wound and he was not seriously hurt. They didn't think I would be charged. But I was past worrying. Way past. After my interview, I was allowed home.

My fury had subsided, but I felt such contempt and disgust at what Bob had said. There was no catharsis, no sense of relief and certainly no remorse. I didn't want him near me. Emma and Becki came round – Bob had called and told them what had happened. He had been totally honest with them and a small part of me felt some grudging respect for him; he was so honest and straightforward in some ways. I was worried the girls might be angry, but instead, they threw their arms around me.

'Something had to give, Mum,' Emma said gently. 'You've been under so much stress.'

Bob showed up the following day. The door banged and he stood in the kitchen, looking ten years older. I wasn't sure what to say; I couldn't even look at him. But from behind me, Mum flew at him, hissing, like a wildcat protecting her young.

'If my daughter goes to prison for this, you and I are finished, Downes!' she yelled. 'I want you out of this house, I won't forgive you!'

He looked visibly shaken.

'I shouldn't have said what I said,' he mumbled.

It was the nearest I'd get to an apology. I looked at him and saw the pain and anguish and hurt etched on every line of his face. He had suffered, just like me. I knew he hadn't meant what he said – he had lashed out, wanting to hurt me, wanting me to shut up. I had driven him mad, night after night, screaming and ranting about the trial.

'I shouldn't have stabbed you,' I managed.

But it was an uneasy truce. Deep in my heart, there burned a resentment and a hatred, which I knew no amount of apology would ever heal. I wasn't charged, but that really was the least of my worries. Bob, I think, saw it as yet another fresh start for us, a chance to rebuild. But as far as I was concerned there was no chance of that. Much of the love I had for him had been destroyed when Robert went into care. And with this, the last residues were gone.

CHAPTER TWENTY-TWO
HOMECOMING

And so, for whatever reason, I stayed. I knew I was on the verge of a nervous breakdown, but I threw myself into keeping Charlene's name alive. The police and the courts had given up on her, so it was all the more important that my fight carried on. I called the newspapers and the TV stations, but with no more salacious gossip from the trial, their interest had waned. Aimlessly, I wandered around Blackpool, down dark side streets and alleyways, unsure of what exactly I was looking for until I found it. I built myself up into walking down 'Paki Alley'. Was I retracing her last steps? Did my little girl skip down this very pavement to her death?

'Charlene,' I whispered, 'where are you?'

But the only reply was the sound of tinny teenage music, blaring out from the takeaways, and workers cursing in languages I didn't understand. They were laughing too and that hurt me even more. Nobody even gave me a second glance as I stood on the street and my tears flowed. It was a lonely battle, and one I knew I could not win. Empty and aching inside, I trudged home.

I was fighting hard for Robert too. Now 16, he was a young adult and so I began pleading with social services to allow him to come home.

'It's where he belongs,' I insisted. 'He wants to be with us. Please.'

Robert was desperate – he had hated every minute of his time in care. Besides, it wasn't as if they had made any progress with his behaviour at all. In fact, he was more of a challenge than he had ever been; climbing out of the windows at night, running away, getting into fights. If anyone mentioned Charlene to him, he would go off like a firework. And some of the other lads at the home knew just how to wind him up, so he was always in trouble. The social workers were struggling to cope with him.

'Let me try,' I begged. 'I am his mum, after all.'

It sounded like a weak excuse, as if that counted for nothing, but I kept on badgering them, calling his social workers every day. Robert was pleading with them from his end too. Eventually, they agreed to a trial period.

'Let's see how it goes for the first month or so,' they said. 'We'll bring him home next week.'

'Yes!' I whooped, running around the living room, the phone still in my hand. I was very excited – but strangely nervous too. I couldn't actually allow myself to believe it would go as planned; I felt that I was tempting fate. We'd had so much heartache and bad luck and let-downs, it was difficult to accept that this time something wonderful was going to happen.

On the day of Robert's homecoming, I was up early, and I washed his Liverpool quilt and cleaned and aired his room. I'd bought bacon, eggs, thick white bread and lots of treats. I couldn't wait. Like a caged tiger, waiting for one of her cubs to come home, I paced the floor. And when the door opened, and he walked, uncertain at first, into the kitchen, I was overcome by an outpouring of raw emotion. I grabbed him and we sobbed together. Bob came into the kitchen and there was an awkward, formal sort of embrace between the two of them.

'All right, Dad?' Robert said gruffly.

I could see Bob was smarting, but I didn't know what else he could expect. He had let his son down. Hugely. And the wounds would take a lifetime to heal. The relationship between the two of them was strained, but I didn't let that spoil my happiness at having my beloved son home. Within days, Robert's bedroom was a tip – clothes everywhere, dirty socks, even bike parts. He and Bob were keen cyclists and Robert had decided to strip and rebuild an old bike he'd found in the shed.

'Not in your bedroom!' I chided. 'There's oil everywhere!'

Secretly, I was absolutely thrilled. On my hands and knees, I scrubbed at the oil stains on his carpet with a feeling of contentment: it was so good to feel useful and needed again. I didn't really care if he poured oil all over the house. I'd missed all those habits, even the bad ones; I'd missed all the cleaning and ironing and cooking too. I'd missed being a mum.

'I'm so glad to be home,' he told me.

My eyes brimmed with tears and I felt closer to being happy than I ever had since the day Charlene vanished. At weekends, I'd rustle up his favourite, a bacon and egg toastie. And I didn't complain when he dripped sauce on the table or wiped his greasy hands on my clean tablecloth – it felt like a privilege, even, to wash his dishes. I had learned the hard way what an honour it was to be a mother – and how I must savour every second of it.

'I'm glad you're home too, son,' I told him. 'More than you could ever know.'

The girls were thrilled to see him back too. Of course there was the usual teasing, criticising his dress sense, pretending to choke on his aftershave. But their faces lit up every time they saw him. Their little brother was home. Yet I could see clearly that Robert was still a very troubled young man. I knew he was struggling and sometimes I wondered whether the pain of being back in Blackpool, surrounded by reminders of Charlene, was worse than being away. I caught him, more than once, standing on the landing outside Charlene's room, perhaps too afraid of his own reaction to go inside. She was everywhere in the house: her photos were on the walls, her candle burned by her window. And that constant reminder could be a curse as well as a comfort, I knew only too well myself.

Robert was more similar to Bob than probably he liked to admit. The two of them bottled up their feelings. He wasn't the sort to give me a cuddle or confide his troubles in me. Instead, he'd go off out with his mates, go missing for hours, and stagger home later, stinking of booze.

'You're drinking too much,' I remonstrated. 'I'm worried about you, think of your health.'

But he just growled at me. After the euphoria of coming home, he always seemed so tense now, so loaded with pent-up aggression – as if he was just about to blow at any moment. I could understand why people were wary of him. He was loyal and caring towards me, but I knew I was probably the only person who was safe from his temper.

One evening, just after 9pm, Robert came home bristling with anger, specks of blood on his clothes.

'What happened?' I demanded.

'I went into Tesco Express to buy a sandwich and a bottle of pop,' he told me. 'And I bumped into Mohammed Raveshi on my way out.'

My heart sank: even the sound of his name sent a chill through me.

'What did you do?' I asked nervously.

'I punched him full in the face and he fell over,' Robert told me calmly. 'Well, I couldn't just let him walk past me, could I?'

I was stunned at how blasé he was, but I pushed those thoughts aside. My only focus was to protect my son, at whatever cost, and so I stripped his clothes off and bundled them into the washing machine quickly.

'Get yourself upstairs,' I said hurriedly. 'Out of the way. Let me deal with this.'

I knew what was coming next. Sure enough, there was a knock at the door soon afterwards and I spotted a police car outside. My heart was pounding; I wasn't sure I had it in me to tell a lie to the police. Already I could feel myself sweating and blushing, before I'd even started. And yet I couldn't let them take my son away – not again. None of this was his fault, this wasn't the real Robert. I opened the door, undecided what to do, but to my surprise Robert appeared at my shoulder and spoke first.

'Yes, I hit him,' he said. 'I hold my hands up.'

My heart sank. I had to admit, I was deeply disappointed that he had told the truth. It was a shameful position to be in as a mother. But then, I was used to that by now – self-criticism came very easily to me. More than anything, I wanted to keep my son safe. I had failed Charlene, I couldn't fail him too.

'He's lived with this since he was a child,' I reminded the officers. 'Please go easy on him.'

I watched from Charlene's window as Robert got into the police car, as though he was hopping into the back of a taxi. This had become a way of life for him. And I wondered, not for the first time, if he was too far gone to be rescued.

It was the early hours before he came home, but I was still wide awake. But that just worried me even more. It wasn't the actual attack – it was his reaction to it – that kept me awake at night.

Robert appeared before Blackpool Magistrates' Court in March 2012 and admitted assault. The court heard Mohammed Raveshi had suffered a damaged eye and had needed hospital treatment. The defence barrister told the court that Robert 'took one swing at him, hardly breaking his stride as he did so'.

Robert was sentenced to a 12-month supervision order, which was designed to address his anger management issues. The judge seemed to show him compassion and said: 'These were an extremely unusual and unfortunate set of circumstances.'

I was so thankful that he wasn't jailed. But again, what worried me most was that Robert hardly seemed concerned by the outcome. Violence had become the first response for my son. For him, fighting was as normal and as necessary as cleaning his teeth. And I wondered where it would end.

Robert drank more and more. He hooked up with his old school pals and they'd go round all the Blackpool pubs, every weekend, more often than not getting into some sort of scrape. Occasionally, he would give me a glimpse of his turmoil and my heart would splinter and shatter all over again.

'I look for Charlene everywhere I go,' he told me. 'Some nights, I walk up and down the pier, looking for her. I've been in every takeaway, every arcade.

'Funny thing is, I'm looking for a 14-year-old girl. I can't imagine her any getting any older.'

I nodded sadly; I knew just what he meant. Perhaps Charlene would be 14 forever, always our little girl.

One morning, around a year after he came home, Robert went out and I didn't hear from him all day so when the police knocked on my door, my stomach hit the floor. I expected them to tell me he'd been in yet another fight.

'I'm afraid we found your son on the end of the pier,' said an officer. 'He's been taken to hospital, but he'd like to see you.'

I stared at him in alarm.

'Is he injured?' I asked. 'What's happened?'

'He was found trying to hang himself,' he replied. 'We managed to cut him down and he's OK, but he needs some help.'

My blood ran cold. Charlene had disappeared on the North Pier and now, Robert had tried to hang himself there. My head was swimming, spinning.

I was the only one at home and I didn't want to call mum or the girls to worry them – not until I knew what was going on. I got a cab to Blackpool Victoria Hospital and found Robert in a side room. He could hardly lift his head to face me.

'I'm sorry, Mum,' he mumbled. 'I miss Charlene.'

'I know, son,' I said. 'I know.'

With his head in his hands, Robert told me he had tried to hang himself, in the darkness, on the pier, but someone walking on the beach below had spotted him. The police and coastguard had rushed to save him.

'That's Charlene, looking after you,' I said softly. 'She saved you. You must never do this again.'

But Robert couldn't make any promises, I knew that: my poor boy was broken and I didn't know how to fix him. He was assessed by the mental health team, but they decided he was not ill enough to be sectioned. Instead, he was sent home with the promise of counselling and support.

That night, long after he had gone to bed, I paced the landing, checking on him, my heart heavy with anxiety. I felt like he was 12 years old, all over again, and he was climbing out of the windows to look for his sister. The years had passed, but really, nothing had changed. And though my son was home, I knew that he was very far away. I watched him like a hawk, checking his pockets, searching his room, always with the gnawing worry in the back of my mind that he might try it again.

'You can't watch him 24 hours a day,' Mum said. 'You have to let him go.'

But I couldn't – I almost worried about him more now than I had when he was away. He was bound to come face-to-face with Albattikhi and Raveshi again at some point and I dreaded to think what he might do to them.

And then, it happened with Emma, too. In December 2008, she went on a night out with some friends and she came across Albattikhi in a local nightclub. They rowed, words were exchanged and her temper flared. She slapped him across the face and tried to slap him a second time, but he grabbed her hand. In September 2009, she too was hauled before magistrates, where she admitted assaulting him.

'I'm not sorry,' Emma seethed. 'He spat at me before I slapped him.'

The case appeared in all the newspapers. It seemed like every mistake my family made – every bad thing that happened – was plastered all over the media. And it hurt all the more that those same newspapers wouldn't print a single word in support of my daughter when we needed them so desperately.

* * *

Five months after the trial was abandoned, I decided to hold a memorial service for Charlene. Far from dreading the day, I really looked forward to it: I wanted a chance to celebrate her life. In my heart, there was always hope, but the rational voice inside my head would tell me she was dead, that she would never have her 18th and 21st birthdays, her graduation, her wedding day. I feared she would never even have a funeral.

What kind of mother would wish for her daughter's funeral?

And yet for me, it would mean that I could least honour her memory. A funeral would mean dignity and peace – and the end of hope. Yet I didn't have that cruellest luxury of burying my own child. So, this was to be her day.

The service was held at St John's Church, in September 2008, in the centre of Blackpool, and attended by senior police officers, friends and family. I chose 'Soledad,' a song by Westlife to open the service – Charlene had loved the band. I remembered her singing noisily along as we drove from Coventry to Blackpool, her heart full of excitement, her future full of promise. How could I have known I was driving her to her death? We sang 'The Lord's My Shepherd' too. It was one of my favourite hymns. And at the end, Puff Daddy's 'I'll be Missing You'.

'There will always be hope,' I told the congregation. 'Always.'

Robert and Becki gave readings. And a lovely lady called Marie McCourt read a poem called 'God's Lent Child' – Marie had contacted me after she had read about Charlene in the press. Her own daughter, Helen, had been murdered in 1988, at the age of 22. Though her killer, Ian Simms, was jailed, Helen's body was never found. Marie had dedicated the rest of her life to campaigning for killers who refused to reveal the whereabouts of a body to be refused parole. She wanted Simms to be charged with preventing her daughter's burial and was a member of a group called Support Against Murder and Manslaughter (SAMM).

'There are people at the group, like you, like me,' she told me kindly. 'People who wait. People who hope. People who grieve.'

She and I were different women but we bonded. The pain etched across her face was all too familiar to me and her humanity and compassion gave me a feeling of comfort and belonging. When she agreed to attend Charlene's service, I was so touched. The world was full of cranks and madmen and often they grabbed the attention and the headlines, but there were nuggets of golden kindness to be found too.

In December 2008, we were invited to an annual service, held by SAMM, at Liverpool Cathedral. Becki and I got the train together and made our way towards the cathedral, like pilgrims, carrying heavy burdens. We prayed and wept with other families who, like us, had had their hearts and souls ripped out. I realised, if I was to cope, as the mother of a missing child, I would need to draw on this strength and support. Charlene's memorial service had given me a focus and a purpose, a reason to get up each morning. It was almost as though I was keeping my daughter alive, bringing her a little closer to me, as I had done in those early days. I decided I would like somewhere to go, where I could talk to her – somewhere peaceful, there was no grave. When I told Marie, she suggested: 'Why don't you get a memorial bench? We have a bench for my daughter.'

'That's perfect,' I replied. 'Everyone will remember her then.'

And so I began thinking about a fundraiser – a sponsored walk maybe, or a fun day. I wasn't sure what to do. But then Becki came home with good news.

'I've got funding for the bench,' she announced.

She was a member of a support group called Connex-ions, a type of youth committee in Blackpool, and they had offered to pay for the bench.

I was truly grateful – I didn't even know these people, but yet again, shining bright amongst the evil and the apathy, we had stumbled across a gem of kindness. And it warmed my heart.

'Where do you want it?' Becki asked. 'We need to choose a place that's special to us all.'

We had so many lovely memories of Charlene. They nestled safe in my mind, but I was almost scared to pick through them. The pain, the longing, for what once had been, was often best kept shut away.

'Mum, what about that day we went to Morecambe?' Becki asked with a smile.

I allowed myself to think back and found myself smiling. Charlene had been about 12 when we'd taken the kids for a day out; Mum came along too. She had her photo taken, with Becki, next to the famous Eric Morecambe statue. We went on the fair and Charlene turned a shade of green as she spun this way and that on the waltzers, but afterwards, she had laughed and begged for another turn.

'I won't be sick, I promise,' she told me. 'I love it.'

Another summer, we'd all gone off to Southport for the day. There was a fairground there too and Becki, Char-lene and Robert had been on just about every ride.

'Come on, Mummy, why don't you have a go?' Charlene cajoled. 'And you too, Nanna!'

There was a glint of mischief in her eyes and I found myself nodding and agreeing – even though I hated any kind of ride. Before I knew it, Mum and I were clinging on, inside a cable car, as it rose steadily higher above the town. As I screamed in absolute terror, I looked down to see Becki, Charlene and Robert, howling with laughter and pointing up at us. My stomach was doing somersaults but it was worth it to see the looks on the children's faces.

'Never again!' I spluttered, when we finally got back on the ground.

Mum was so dizzy, Bob had to link her arm. The kids thought it was hilarious. We bought chips on the way home, and Charlene and Robert fell asleep on the back seat of the car, their toes full of sand, hair sticky with candyfloss. It had been a good day out, one of the best.

And then, of course, there was our family favourite – Stanley Park. Charlene had loved it there too.

Charlene loves *it there, Karen*, I reminded myself silently. *Getting a bench doesn't mean you have to talk about her in the past.*

When was that? When did a missing child become past tense? Was there an official date on which to give up hope? A tear trickled down my cheek and Becki squeezed my hand.

'Let's concentrate on the bench, Mum,' she said.

I nodded. At Stanley Park, there was a big lake, with ducks and geese, and rowing boats. There was a play area, a running track, football pitches and tennis courts. In summer, Bob would often take the children to feed the ducks, whilst I caught up on jobs around the house. They'd take crusts from a loaf and any stale biscuits. And then they'd have an ice cream in the sunshine and maybe kick a ball about. Sometimes, if I was in the mood, I'd say: 'Sod the ironing and the cleaning, I'll come with you. There's no medals for housework!'

One time, Bob had hired a rowing boat on the lake. I refused to get in, because I was terrified of water, so the kids all piled in, giggling and rocking the boat. Charlene was screaming because her feet were getting wet, Robert was busy splashing everyone. I watched them, bobbing about amongst the ducks, one rowing one way, one the other. They went around in circles for the whole half-hour. Bob only managed to get them back on dry land with the promise of ice creams and a turn in the penny arcades on our way home.

'I'm dizzy after that,' he complained, as he lifted Robert out of the boat and onto the stones.

But I could tell he'd enjoyed it just as much as they had.

'Can we take one of these ducks home with us?' Charlene had asked. 'They could share my bed?'

I had laughed and scooped her up in my arms, and I had felt that our happiness, and our security, would last forever.

'Let's put her bench there,' I said.

'Stanley Park is perfect,' Becki agreed. And Bob felt the same.

The new bench had a plaque, bearing Charlene's name, and would be anchored down, just at the edge of the water, where the ducks gathered.

'Charlene loved those ducks,' I said fondly. 'She'd like it there, she *will* like it there.'

We planned a small ceremony, just for family and friends, when the bench was ready. It was a cold afternoon, in early spring 2009, but I wanted us all to make an effort. The vicar came and sprinkled some holy water, before blessing the bench.

'May you find comfort here,' she said to me.

And I did. I often went to sit on the bench, just to talk to Charlene and throw some bread to the ducks. I'd hear the wind rustling in the reeds around the water's edge and I fancied I could hear her giggling.

'I'm here for you, darling,' I whispered.

CHAPTER TWENTY-THREE
MOVING HOUSE

I still yearned for Charlene's smell, her touch, the sound of her laughter, in the house. I often felt troubled too; almost haunted. In every corner, I saw wispy shadows; I heard whispers in her bedroom. Sometimes, I could smell roses – pink ones were her favourite flowers. And I was torn. I wanted my daughter, but I wanted to think of Charlene as she once was, not as she might be now. In the early hours, with the house deathly quiet, the words of the psychic would come back to trouble me. I wanted to wipe my memory, forget the psychic. Forget what was said at the trial. But it was impossible.

Long after the barristers and the journalists had forgotten my daughter's name, I was wide-eyed with lunacy, night after night, going over the horrific things they had said. It weighed so heavily on my mind and I began to dread being in the house on my own. Robert wasn't at home much, and though he didn't say, I knew that he found it hard too, sleeping next door to Charlene's old room, seeing her posters on the wall, her teddies on the bed. Mum was often out seeing her pals and she'd go to bed early. So, mostly, it was just Bob and me, rattling around, barely speaking, painfully conscious of the silence, the crushing sense of hopelessness.

'Can we move, Bob?' I asked eventually. 'I really can't bear this any more. The house is too big, it's too sad.'

But I didn't want a fresh start – that almost implied we were leaving Charlene behind. I didn't want to move far either, just in case she came home; I needed to be nearby. So I asked our landlord, and he told us he had a smaller house, just a five-minute walk away.

'It's worth a try,' I decided.

But packing up was hard. I could barely bring myself to go through Charlene's things – her school uniform, her school books. There was her old blazer and a frayed tie. I held them close and smelled them: she was still there, but it was so faint. I even came across her missing Reebok trainer, white and gold (she'd lost it just before she'd disappeared). I remembered her moaning about it as she finished off poached eggs that morning.

Oh, such petty worries, such treasured memories!

'It's here, Charlene, you silly thing,' I said softly. 'Here all along.'

I had the trainer – but where was my daughter? In the new house, she still had a room, shared with my mum, with her belongings in a box by the bed. I wanted everything ready for her – just in case. I still had hope. While my heart was still beating, I would always have hope. We arranged her teddies on the chest of drawers in a long line.

'She'll be OK in here with me,' Mum reassured me. 'Don't worry, Karen.'

But I couldn't bear to unpack the Darren Day posters, I couldn't even look at those. They were kept safe for the day – whenever it came – when she could put them up herself. Of course, when she came home, she might be too grown-up, too mature for all those cuddly toys. But I doubted it somehow. And I couldn't imagine she would ever out-grow Darren Day. She'd love him forever, she'd once told me. And I believed her.

'It's nice here,' Mum said. 'You've done the right thing.'

But even she didn't sound convinced. And it was hard to settle in the new house. I found myself missing the ghostly giggles, the creaking doors, the mere suggestion, maybe no more than a butterfly on a windowsill, that Charlene was there. I missed her window too. I had put myself through unspeakable agony sitting at that window, hour after hour, year after year; I had wanted to purge myself of it. Saying goodbye to the house, to the window, I had almost felt a sense of relief, of defiance.

I had suffered so much there and, irrational though it was, I blamed the bricks and mortar and the glass panes. But now, I longed for it. It had become a part of me, synonymous with my Charlene and with my hope. And I yearned to have it back.

* * *

Less than a year on, still restless, we were on the move again, this time to another little terrace nearby. Again, Charlene's belongings came with us, to share a room with Mum. From here, through the upstairs window, I could actually see our old family home. This was such a comfort to me; if she came home – *when* she came home – I would be the first to see her. The car park, where she and Martin once played, was now a supermarket. Martin was a young man now, but seemed so lost and haunted still. He hadn't been able to settle at a job. So much had changed. The world had moved on, but not me. For hours, I would stand and stare out of the bedroom windows, onto the streets below, and imagine Charlene walking home, with her sisters, her hands in theirs. Maybe they'd have a bag of chips, or a milkshake each. Maybe some new clothes from the shops on the promenade. Or perhaps she'd be on her bike, cycling alongside Becki, chattering as fast as she was pedalling.

Just a stone's throw away, over the rooftops, was the North Pier – a glaring fault line between our old life and the new. Down one street was the row of tawdry take-aways. Who knew what unspeakable horrors lay hidden behind those gaudy shopfronts? The lights of the amusement arcades twinkled in the distance. Once, they had seemed so inviting, exciting. Now it seemed they were luring children in, trapping them and swallowing them whole. I could see, too, the infamous 'Paki Alley' and it made me shudder. We had thought we were moving to Las Vegas, but this was the stuff nightmares were made of – and my Charlene, my daughter, was lost in it all.

I pulled the curtains shut and turned away from the window.

No more, I told myself.

In this new house, there was a self-contained flat upstairs. Without any actual discussion, Bob took the upstairs flat and Mum and I had the ground floor. I still cooked his meals, washed his clothes, cleaned his shoes. We were all but separated – hanging on together, by the thinnest of threads, for the sake of our missing child. I kept out of his way as much as I could; I looked after Mum and Robert, I prayed at the little chapel. And I loved going to Barnardo's too, where I'd done the parenting course before Charlene went missing. That all felt like another universe now, but I'd kept in touch with some of the volunteers there and I'd made some good friends.

'You really ought to apply for Criminal Injury Compensation,' they told me. 'You're entitled to it.'

I shook my head, at first appalled by the idea.

'I don't want money, it doesn't seem right,' I said firmly.

'Look, the money is there for people like you,' they reasoned. 'Other people claim, why shouldn't you?'

That got me thinking. After all, Bob and I struggled for money. Now that was an understatement – I hadn't been able to go back to work after Charlene vanished. Bob had tried, but he found it hard too. It would be nice to be able to treat the children, maybe pay for them to go on holiday. Money wouldn't solve anything, but it always helped. It was autumn 2009 when I made an appointment with a solicitor and Bob and I both went along. It took just one quick consultation and three months later, we received £5,500 each from the Criminal Injuries Compensation Authority. Seeing the amount, in black and white on a cheque, made me recoil.

'I don't want it,' I said immediately.

It seemed abhorrent, as though I was accepting the money in exchange for Charlene.

'This doesn't make it all OK,' I protested. 'I want my daughter, I don't want this cheque.'

Besides, I had no idea how they had reached such a figure either. The amount didn't matter. But then of course it did, because it seemed in some way to reflect her value.

And like all children, she was priceless. In the end, I cashed the cheque and shared it out between our three remaining children. I had no idea what Bob did with his share and I wasn't overly interested.

I pushed the payment to the back of my mind, just as I did my best not to think of the two men who had been tried in connection with my daughter's death. The bile that was spewed on the secret tapes had seeped into our lives like a cancer. I began to think it might kill me if I didn't shut it out.

Soon after our payout, a police officer called to see us.

'What is it this time?' I asked wearily.

Hesitantly, he explained that the two defendants had both made an application for compensation and they were expected to receive in the region of £250,000 each. The poor man hadn't finished his sentence before Bob exploded.

'It's disgraceful!' he yelled. 'Get out of my f***ing house!'

But the police officer was used to Bob by now and calmly carried on.

'We don't necessarily agree with the payment, but we can't do anything about it. I just thought you should know.'

I nodded, numb: they were not guilty of anything, it was important to remember that. It wasn't that I wanted anything either. But I, as Charlene's mother, had been awarded £5,500. The money was an afterthought, incidental. But for the defendants to receive such a huge payout seemed obscene. It felt as though there was nobody, nobody at all, on our side. Like a cheap suit, the police investigation had fallen apart at the seams.

* * *

In October 2009, I bought a copy of the *Blackpool Gazette* and froze at the headline. An investigation by the Independent Police Complaints Commission (IPCC) had been published. It was a shock, yet another one. Nobody had even thought to let me know there was an investigation, or that it was going to be made public. But then, I was used to that by now – I was just Charlene's mother and nobody in authority seemed to think that counted. I read each word feverishly and it was even more damning than I could have imagined. It left me reeling with shock and anger that my daughter had been failed so blatantly. The report ruled that the investigation into Charlene's death had been so full of errors that they could result in the killer never being found. I had suspected that, right from the moment the second trial was abandoned, but to see it written down, in an official document, was so final.

The IPCC said the investigation was 'handled poorly and unprofessionally' and that the evidence contained a 'catalogue of errors which undermined the court case'. The watchdog recommended one officer should face a disciplinary hearing, another should receive a written warning and five others should receive words of advice.

Sobbing, I went home to show Bob.

'How come they didn't tell us this?' he asked forlornly.

It wasn't like him to be so subdued. But I understood that, like me, he was defeated and broken.

We had to follow what happened next through our local paper – just like everyone else.

And later, following the review, Detective Sergeant Jan Beasant, a detective who had worked on the case, was found guilty of two counts of misconduct at a disciplinary hearing in December 2011. She was forced to resign. Lancashire Police said Ms Beasant had shown conduct that 'let everyone down'. Ms Beasant had the job of transcribing secretly recorded conversations between Albattikhi and another man, and she had spent 2,500 hours over two years listening to 52 audio tapes. At the trial the quality of the recordings was criticised by defence barristers as 'poor' and confidence was 'low' in the accuracy of the transcriptions. The IPCC concluded the investigating team were guilty of a strategic and tactical failure in the management of the material. Naseem Malik, IPCC Commissioner for the North West, said it was 'abundantly clear' that the covert surveillance had been 'handled poorly and unprofessionally'. Superintendent Simon Giles said the force 'expects the highest professional standards from all our staff and the panel has found this individual's conduct has fallen well short of these standards.'

He added: 'This sort of behaviour and conduct lets everybody down – not just the police service, but those the police serve. It is appropriate they have faced the consequences of their actions.'

'The entire investigation is like a car crash,' I sighed, folding up the latest report in the newspaper and squashing it into the kitchen bin. 'One problem after another.'

And so it went on. Ms Beasant later claimed she was made a scapegoat for failings in the investigation and she was cleared of any wrongdoing in connection with the investigation into Charlene's disappearance. A police tribunal said she should be reinstated. A second officer, Don Fraser, suspended in 2011, announced his intention to sue. Mr Fraser, who was employed as a civilian worker by Lancashire Police after earlier retiring as a constable, had faced a disciplinary hearing, but he quit the force just days before the hearing and launched a claim for constructive dismissal.

It seemed like one catastrophic mistake after another. And we were left to read about it all in the media, as if we were no more than passing tourists. The whole sordid mess had cost a fortune. Careers were ruined, lives shattered. And the more we dug for the truth, the further away it got. The amount of money paid out in relation to the investigation, the failings and the mistakes was staggering, truly repugnant. It seemed like everyone was making a few quid out of our tragedy. Charlene had been completely lost in the arguments of the trial. And now, she was lost in the complaints and the payouts.

'It's not right,' I said sadly. 'It's not right that a child should be forgotten like this.'

CHAPTER TWENTY-FOUR
A DESPERATE MOTHER

We were no nearer finding her than on the day she had disappeared. Far from wanting to right the wrongs of their investigation, I felt like the police wanted to sweep it all under the carpet. It was as if there was no one who cared about Charlene, no one willing to help us in any way. I was so, so desperate for help, and utterly despairing at the complete lack of justice for my daughter. It was at this point, at the start of 2011, when I felt so devastated at the lack of police support, the lack of justice for my murdered daughter, that I was contacted by a man called Tommy Robinson.

He was from the EDL, the English Defence League, an organisation I had never heard of before. I told him so, and in return, he told me that he wanted to arrange a protest in Charlene's name to appeal for justice. I couldn't believe it – here was this random stranger offering to help get the word out there, offering more than anyone else had done for me. He asked me to attend, and I said yes – I didn't have time to research Tommy and, frankly, I didn't want to. I didn't want to know more about this man, I wanted to find a way to get Charlene's name out there, into the world, so that I could finally achieve some sort of justice for her. I was so grateful for any support that I didn't care who was offering it.

That same week, a couple of police officers called round.

'Are you planning on attending the EDL march?' they asked.

'Yes, I am,' I said, surprised they even knew about it.

'We're concerned about it,' they told me. 'We don't want things to get out of hand.'

'These people want to help me, they want justice for Charlene,' I said.

The police officers seemed hesitant, but by now I was way past putting my trust in them. I went ahead and attended the protest. I know the EDL hold beliefs that I absolutely, in no way, agree with. But let me ask you this – if you were being offered something that should have been offered to you by the police and the courts, would you take it? If you had lost a child, in such a terrible and horrific way, would you accept all the help you could get, to try and achieve a sliver of what the judiciary system had failed to achieve for you and your family?

On the day itself, in May 2011, I didn't know what to expect and I was nervous. As I reached the crowd, I realised this was far bigger than I had expected. There were hundreds upon hundreds of protestors, many of them wearing: 'Justice For Charlene' T-shirts. In total, I was told there were 2,000 people, all gathered together for my daughter. I was overwhelmed – I couldn't believe so many people had come out.

The next day, I hurried out to the newsagent's and Charlene's photo was on the front page of our local newspaper – exactly what I had wanted to happen. The world was finally listening. Now I know the EDL had their own political message to spread and they weren't helping me out of the goodness of their hearts. There was another protest, which Becki attended with me. At the end of it, Charlene's name was in the newspapers once again; she was even on TV. Word spread of our fight for justice. This was all I ever wanted.

I was staggered by the huge police presence in Blackpool and I reminded myself bitterly how few officers had been allocated to look for Charlene when she went missing. There was a ring of steel around the takeaways and the alleyways and it incensed me.

What about protecting our children instead?

I learned more and more about the seedy side of the town we once loved. There were claims of highly organised grooming gangs, involving as many as 60 young girls. It was said that sex abuse in the town was endemic, claimed that Blackpool was fast becoming a haven for sex abusers, because of low-cost housing and the seasonal, unskilled work on offer. To me, it felt like the whole sordid story was being covered up, layer upon layer, as the victims sank deeper and deeper into the dirt. And my Charlene was buried at the very bottom. But this was no longer just about my daughter – there were lots of other girls involved. Some of them were still being abused, some could still be saved.

'It's too late for my daughter, but not for them,' I vowed.

It gave me a sense of purpose, a reason to go on. If I could campaign for other children in Charlene's name, it would be the most wonderful legacy.

* * *

Through the police I was introduced to Sue McGurty, who ran an organisation called Mosac, Mothers (and safe carers) of sexually abused children in Blackpool and the district.

'I'm working to protect children like Charlene,' she told me.

I was so desperate for help, for anyone to help me, that I also met with the then leader of the British National Party (BNP), Nick Griffin. By then I had learned not to rely on the reliable, and instead to expect help in the most unexpected of places. In fact, I was willing to listen to anyone. I was interviewed by Nick in October 2011 on Charlene's memorial bench and I was angry that the only people offering help were those who of course had their own agenda to serve. As we sat, children were laughing and splashing about in the rowing boats, toddlers were feeding ducks, families were enjoying ice creams. For a moment, I gulped in the scene, remembering our other life, our days out here. I imagined I could almost hear Charlene giggling too.

I snapped back to reality. Nick spoke of the Asian grooming gangs and the dozens of girls in Blackpool apparently caught up in the abuse. As the water lapped on the pebbles nearby, a wave of guilt washed over me and I covered my face. I knew how it looked: my 14-year-old daughter had a secret life I knew nothing about. But that was the truth – I just hadn't known. Did that make me a bad mother? I was certainly a mother who had made mistakes, of that I was in no doubt at all.

Years earlier, I wouldn't have opened my door to people like Nick Griffin and Tommy Robinson. But now I was a different woman in a different time and this trauma was all mine. And so the pomposity of people bothered me very little. It was always the most sanctimonious of twits who were ready to condemn but weren't actually prepared to offer any help themselves. Anxious not to offend the offenders, they didn't seem to give two hoots about the victims. I was a mother without a child. And that combination – or lack of it – is a lethal one. I was prepared to go to any lengths, to work with anyone, and to try anything.

Predictably, the two movements ended up like squabbling children and there was no way I was going to let my fight for Charlene get bogged down in their politics. One of the final things the BNP did for my campaign for justice was to set up a meeting for me with Nazir Afzal, the North West's Chief Crown Prosecutor. He was, I was told, famous for campaigning on issues around child sexual exploitation.

But when I got to Manchester for our meeting in September 2013, Mr Afzal wasn't expecting us at all – we had to chase after him as he came out onto the street. When we caught him up, he seemed a very approachable and reasonable man. But after talking to him for a little while, he said: 'I am very much aware of Charlotte's case.'

At this my hackles rose. Couldn't he even get her name right? It was a small slip-up, but to me, fiercely protective – and always now driven to be on the defensive – I felt this was yet another sign that my daughter didn't matter, that a working-class girl from a chaotic and problematic background just did not count. At the same time, the support and the money was pouring in for the search for Madeleine McCann. I had read that her parents had been to meet with the Home Secretary, Theresa May, in London. Meanwhile, I had to chase officials up the street to get noticed. My daughter had no voice. And quite literally, it seemed, no name.

The next day, my meeting with Mr Afzal was uploaded to a YouTube channel and the response was huge. A reporter from *The Times* knocked on my door and asked why I was working with the BNP.

'I can't get Theresa May to see me, so the BNP will have to do!' I snapped. 'And until the bloody BBC start showing an interest, I will have to make do with YouTube to get my point across!'

I was so angry. No one wanted to help me, it seemed. The reporter didn't seem to understand that he and his sort were both the cause of the problem and the solution. If my Charlene had been able to play the piano and write in Latin, I felt sure his big newspaper with the small writing would have been so much more sympathetic to us, so much earlier. As it was, I didn't understand much of the vocabulary it used and most of my shopping was own-brand labels so I was stuck with the BNP. I was a political pawn, I could see that – I wasn't quite as stupid as the mainstream media thought. But what on earth was wrong with being a pawn if it helped me to find my daughter? That was the only thing I wanted – it's what anyone would want.

* * *

I was clutching at straws, still. But I was desperate to explore every avenue I could and so at the end of 2013, the BNP put me in touch with a famous psychic called Carol Everett, who had worked on missing persons' cases before. She'd appeared on TV many times and had a lot of successes. Carol was based in Spain and so I was asked to send her a brief email, along with a photo of Charlene. I chose her school picture, where she was smiling, her cheeks chubby, her eyes full of innocence – I loved that one. I waited, wondering what the answer would say. When it came, by email, I scanned the paragraphs, my heart thumping, looking for good news that I knew wasn't there.   Carol said she believed Charlene was dead. And her explanation of where Charlene's body lay was so detailed, it took my breath away. She had even drawn a picture of the location and believed Charlene was in a place with bluebells and streams, near a church and overlooking a learning centre, where there were games being played. It sounded so peaceful and restful that I half-smiled. The place was, she said, between three and ten miles away. I thought hard; I could think of nowhere like that. But then, the writing became more grisly. She claimed that Charlene had been taken away in a white refrigerator van, in black bags, by up to three men.

'They have taken off her head,' she wrote.

My blood ran cold. This was exactly what the first psychic, Sheila, had said: my poor Babby had been beheaded. At this I burst into tears and slapped my laptop shut – I couldn't bear to read that email and yet I knew it could be vital. I called the police and begged them to employ a psychic.

'They do it in America,' I told them desperately.

'We're not in America,' they replied.

And that was that.

So I set up a website in Charlene's name: 'Justice For Charlene'. It was a chance to send her name and her story across the world. Who knew what news or leads might come of it? I had positive messages from friends and strangers alike, and keeping up with all the mail kept me busy – it was good for me. Finally, I felt like I had a purpose and that I was doing something to try and bring my daughter home.

CHAPTER TWENTY-FIVE

A NEW LOVE

One day, in April 2012, I got a message from a man called Mark Bailey, in New Zealand.

'It must have been awful for you,' he wrote. 'You poor woman. I don't know how you've stayed so strong.'

Mark told me he worked as a professional pianist and his life could not have been more different to mine. He still lived with his mum, to whom he wasn't close. He was an only child and had been very lonely. Instead of playing with friends, he had played the piano, daily, since he was four years old.

'I suppose my piano was there instead of a friend,' he told me sadly.

I was a sucker for a sad story and my heart went out to him. As the weeks passed, we talked more and more, and something clicked between us. At first, I chatted about the mundane aspects of my day – my boiler breaking down, Bob grumbling, the constant drizzle of rain in Blackpool. But Mark had a way of making me feel at home, as though I knew him well. Before I realised it, I was confiding in him, telling him about my problems with Bob, about Robert going into care, about my constant, unwavering, agonising desire to see my daughter again.

'I've never met anyone like you,' Mark told me. 'You're amazing.'

I couldn't help but feel flattered. It was many years – longer than I cared to remember – since anyone had noticed me for me. Also, Mark didn't know Charlene. He never would, and that wasn't a bad thing. Full of sympathy, he was genuinely interested in my daughter. But speaking to him was an escape, like time out. I started to really look forward to his messages. And even online – just through a few typed words – he could sense when I was feeling depressed or fed-up. He could pick up more about my mood than Bob, who was sitting across the table from me; he was as sensitive and emotional as Bob was cold and detached. Mark was a trained concert musician, an artist and a performer, so perhaps it was in his nature. I got butterflies every time his name flashed up in my inbox. It was like being a lovesick teenager all over again. I hadn't felt like this since I'd been out rock and roll dancing with Lee, all those years before. And I felt no guilt – my marriage had ended long ago.

'Speaking to you is the best part of my day,' Mark wrote. 'Karen, I've fallen in love with you.'

I stared at the screen, my fingers hovering over the keyboard, unsure how to react. At first his words spooked me. For a start, we had never even met. I hadn't seriously considered him as any kind of boyfriend, he was thousands of miles away. Besides, he was 26, a whopping 21 years younger than me; I even had a little grandson, Riley – Emma's son. Little Riley, born May 23 2011, had brought me so much joy and comfort. Emma was a devoted young mum and as she lived nearby, I saw her and Riley almost every day. I would never know peace again, that was for sure, but my little grandson had certainly taught me to smile. I loved being a grandmother and my dating days were certainly past: I had a complex family and the idea was ridiculous. I had enjoyed a bit of harmless flirting, but this was going too far.

'I want to meet you, to hold you in my arms,' Mark told me. 'I want to play music for you.'

He was so romantic. And I had to admit, I was getting carried along with it all. Even so, his next message was a huge leap forward.

'I've booked my ticket,' he wrote. 'I'm coming to see you.'

I was stunned. He'd spent all his life savings on a flight to Manchester Airport.

This was going too far. My mind spinning, I arranged instead for him to stay with a friend of mine.

In April 2013, I set off to meet Mark at Manchester Airport. I caught a train from Blackpool, after mumbling a half-baked excuse to Bob that I was off to see my god-daughter, Donna Hancock, who was staying in Bolton. Bob barely looked up from his newspaper as I left, and that eased my guilt a little further. But I got hopelessly lost at the airport, and by the time I found the arrivals hall, Mark's flight had landed ages earlier. I spotted him, from behind, sitting on a bench with his case.

'Mark?' I said uncertainly.

I was a bundle of nerves. He turned to me with a big smile – a smile that gave me goose bumps – and said in a rich New Zealand accent: 'Hi babe!' And instantly, I was struck by how young he looked. I was dithering and groaning inwardly, all at once.

Oh God, Karen, what have you done? I wondered inwardly.

Suddenly, I felt very self-conscious and middle-aged. I was dressed like a mum, I looked like a mum – I *was* a mum, for goodness' sake! But Mark behaved, right from that moment, as though we had been in a relationship for months. He kissed and cuddled me, guided me through the crowds, and slipped a protective arm around me.

'This must be strange for you, Karen.' he said, smiling.

As we began chatting, I found myself relaxing a little. Mark was so thrilled to be with me, and I started to feel it too. He made me feel vibrant. Alive. He gushed with compliments and flattery, he was affectionate and loving.

'I'm serious about you, Karen,' he told me.

Far from worrying about things moving too fast, or me being too old, I started to feel younger myself. I still couldn't see how our relationship could work long-term, but I was happy to try. Mark got work easily, playing the piano in a hotel on the promenade.

I got all dressed up to go and listen to him. He was a fantastic pianist; dreamy and sensuous. It was such a pleasure just to hear the keys tinkle under his long, slender fingers – this was like a new lease of life for me. I would walk to meet Mark as plain old Karen Downes and leave as someone totally different. Someone confident, without a past. Or a future. Just living in the now. It was like being Wonderwoman – I had a whole new alter ego.

But I was, of course, worried that someone might see us. By now, my face was well known in Blackpool, as the mum of the missing girl.

The *married* mum of the missing girl.

What will people think? I fretted.

At first, with every flush of happiness, I felt a stab of guilt: I was a grieving mother, it didn't seem right to enjoy myself. What about my Charlene? And of course, there was Bob too. We had a strange relationship that would baffle most people, but he meant something to me all the same. I didn't exactly feel bad, deceiving him, though I did feel uncomfortable. But Mum put me straight with a few words of wisdom.

'Being miserable will not bring Charlene back,' she said gently. 'You're allowed some happiness, Karen. It's OK to smile, it's OK.'

She was right, I realised. Mark would listen for hours when I talked about Charlene. We would take flowers to her memorial bench, together. Out walking, we'd pass the North Pier, with the twinkling lights of the Carousel club, and I'd find myself paralysed by fear and guilt.

'I'm here for you, Karen,' Mark promised.

Though keen to keep him a secret from Bob, I confided in my children.

'I'm glad you're happy.' Emma smiled. 'It sounds like he's good for you, Mum.'

Becki wasn't so sure – she felt there was something fishy about Mark. But I didn't listen to her. She was very over-protective and I reckoned she'd have taken a dislike to anyone I met. Mark had made me smile again and that was something I never would have dreamt possible.

Bob became suspicious as time went on. It would have been impossible, even for someone as impervious as him, not to notice the change in me. One night, I was quickly putting on some make-up, ready to go out, when he came marching into the bathroom.

'What're you getting tarted up for?' he demanded. 'You're too old to be wearing all that stuff, too bloody old!'

Turning from the mirror to face him, suddenly my confidence was dented. I felt deflated.

'Maybe I am and maybe I'm not,' I retorted.

I knew Bob didn't like me dressing up. He didn't like me going out either – there wasn't much he liked, really.

'Who are you going out with, anyway?' he asked.

He was trying hard to sound casual but there was a note of jealousy in his voice. I didn't want to hurt him. More than that, in truth, I didn't want the confrontation.

'I'm meeting a couple of the girls,' I lied. 'Just for a chinwag, you know.'

Bob knew I was lying. *I* knew he knew I was lying. Whether either of us cared so much was another matter: we had a marriage built on sand and it was sinking. I saw Mark as an away day – a ticket away from it all, but a return ticket all the same. He and I had been together for a year when my grandson, Riley, celebrated his third birthday.

'He's having a little party,' I told Mark.

'You're not going there on your own,' he snapped.

I was taken aback.

'You can't come,' I replied. 'It's too soon.'

I tried to explain that I had a family, responsibilities and commitments. It was hard for him to understand, I knew. I could appreciate that he was jealous – I was still living with Bob, after all.

'You have to give me time,' I said.

Mark sulked but I tried to humour him out of it.

'You're worse than a child,' I teased. 'I have to go. You know I do.'

So I went to the party, and afterwards, I met up with Mark in a café. As I checked my phone, he suddenly kicked me under the table.

'Don't check your phone when you're with me!' he ordered.

My leg was stinging, but I was anxious not to make a fuss in public.

'I'm just making sure I haven't missed a call from Mum or my daughters,' I explained. 'Why did you kick me?'

'I don't want you talking to anyone except me,' he retorted.

I didn't understand why he was behaving like that; I went home hurt and confused. As the weeks passed, Mark became increasingly possessive. He put more and more pressure on me to officially leave Bob.

'I want you to move out,' he told me. 'I don't like the thought of you going home to him, night after night.'

But I wasn't ready for that. Bob didn't even know about

Mark and I just couldn't face telling him. Truth was, I didn't want to choose between them. I couldn't – the two men were polar opposites. Mark was my present, maybe my future. He was exciting and young and attractive. But Bob was my past; my children's father, my link to Charlene. Was I naive and selfish to want them both in my life, still?

'Give me a chance to work out what I'm going to do,' I pleaded.

But Mark's whole focus in life seemed to be me. He was getting obsessed. He hadn't made any friends at all since moving to the UK and I felt stifled by his reliance on me. I had so much else to think – and worry – about.

One morning, I was about to set off to Stanley Park, to spend some time at Charlene's bench, when the park warden himself rang me.

'I've got something to tell you,' he said. 'Could you come down to see me? I'm afraid it's not good news.'

I could tell there was something he didn't want to say over the phone. Maybe the bench had been damaged in some way. But when Bob and I arrived, at the edge of the lake, we were horrified: Charlene's bench was half-submerged, in the murky water.

'Vandalised,' said the warden sadly. 'I'm so sorry. It's been ripped up and flung in the water.'

It was another violation of her.

Another twist of the knife.

'Who would do such a cruel thing?' I asked, wringing my hands. There were other benches, many with memorial plaques, dotted around the park, but none of them had been touched. Only Charlene's was targeted.

'Why?' I wept. 'Why do this to her memory?'

The warden was so upset, he was nearly in tears too.

'I'm really sorry,' he kept saying. 'We'll do what we can to help you.'

Bob was shaken up. Back at home, he immediately began making plans to raise money for a new bench. It wasn't like him to be so industrious. Eventually, he settled on the idea of a sponsored bike ride, from Liverpool to Blackpool. He was a keen cyclist, but it was a distance of around 65 miles.

'You're taking on a big commitment there, Bob.'

He had done the distance years before, in aid of a cystic fibrosis charity. But I wasn't sure he could do it again. He was 52 years old, but he'd aged so much since we'd lost Charlene.

'I can do it,' he promised. 'I'll get the money for a new bench, I won't let her down.'

It was so poignant because Charlene, along with Becki, had loved riding her own bike. All the kids had bikes, but it was the two girls who went out after school and cycled up and down the street. Charlene had a little purple bike. I could see her on it now, in my mind's eye.

'She'd like the idea.' I nodded to Bob.

True to his word, he went out training for weeks before-hand, in all weathers, cycling along the promenade from Fleetwood to Lytham St Annes. On the big day, over the summer of 2013, he got the train, with his bike, to Liver-pool and then cycled the whole way back, on his own. On his return, ten hours later, the Lady Mayoress was waiting to greet him at the town hall. I went along too, with the girls. It was tricky, getting away from Mark for the day, but I mumbled something about a bad headache when he called and said I was going back to bed.

'Your dad has done something very special,' I told the girls. 'Let's give him a cheer.'

There was a small crowd of well-wishers, waiting to greet him. But my heart sank when I saw how few local people were there for him. There were many who still suspected, following his arrest and the vicious rumours afterwards, that Bob himself had killed Charlene. And there were even more who didn't believe he was guilty, but they told themselves so, as an excuse not to have to support him and sponsor him. In the end, the bike ride and all his efforts didn't raise enough. Bob was disappointed. We walked home, him wheeling his bike alongside, and he was silent. I sensed his embarrassment and tried to be as kind and as encouraging as I could.

'I'm very proud of you,' I told him awkwardly. 'I know Charlene would be too.'

Back at home, I filled the washing-up bowl with soapy bath suds to soothe his aching feet, but he was so saddle-sore, he could hardly bear to sit down on the couch. He hovered over the cushions, bow-legged, his face crumpled in discomfort. Despite ourselves, we started laughing and I felt a warmth towards him. I was so pleased that he was doing something for Charlene: her daddy was looking out for her. Surely that had to count for something?

And all was not lost with the bench. The park warden called the following week and said his bosses had offered to help with the costs too. The following month, a new bench for Charlene was installed at Carleton Crematorium, under the watchful gaze of swivelling CCTV cameras. I felt uneasy; I wasn't sure she'd like it there so much – it wasn't as peaceful and beautiful as the park. But Bob insisted it was safer there, with security, and I understood it made sense. The local paper ran a story, too, about the new bench, and I was glad of the publicity. It was all about keeping Charlene's name alive. We went to the cremato-rium on special days, with flowers and cards, though it wasn't the same for me, there. Robert would often go and spend a couple of hours sitting and thinking of his sister. On the bus home, he'd scan the crowds for her face.

'I'll never stop looking,' he told me. 'I wish I could.'

CHAPTER TWENTY-SIX
MEMORIAL TURMOIL

It was a burden we would have to carry forever. My only way of coping was to continue organising events and rallies in Charlene's name. On her 23rd birthday, 25th March 2012, we held an open-air service in the rose garden at the crematorium.

We received a plaque to be fixed to her memorial bench. The plaque read: 'Charlene Downes 25.03.89–01.11.03. Gone Too Soon'. I wept when I saw it. The service was beautiful. A soloist, Sarah Eccles, sang 'Something Inside So Strong' by Labi Siffre. We sang 'All Things Bright and Beautiful' and 'The Day Thou Gavest Lord Is Ended'. My friend, Richard, read a poem called 'She Is Gone'. Afterwards, we went onto the promenade, the sea salt stinging our faces, and we watched as balloons were carried on the gusts of wind coming in from the Irish Sea.

I had lost faith, completely, in everything I ever believed in. From the promenade, we went to the police station, with the BNP members, to protest about Charlene's case. Outside, we waved placards and shouted: 'Justice For Charlene.' Horns beeped and people shouted their support as they drove past. But afterwards, walking home, I was overwhelmed by a terrible sadness. With the ten-year anniversary of Charlene's disappearance fast approaching, I wanted to mark the occasion with another memorial service. I spent weeks planning, organising and sending out invitations.

'I want to come to the service,' Mark whined. 'I want to be there with you.'

'No,' I said firmly. 'This is about Charlene, not you. Let me concentrate on my daughter.'

Mark was put out, I could tell. But I was so anxious to make sure the service went well, I hardly gave him a thought. A few days later, Bob's Aunt Bet visited from Coventry and I was busy making her a brew when the doorbell rang. It was a reporter I vaguely recognised from a national broadsheet newspaper.

'Can I come in?' he asked. 'We're going to publish an article about Charlene.'

So I invited him inside as any publicity was good for our case.

I could see he was very well-to-do and I was very conscious of my Midlands accent, of the shabby sofa he was sitting on and the layer of dust on the fireplace. I was on the backfoot before he even spoke. And then he said: 'We believe you moved to Blackpool from The Midlands because Charlene was about to be taken into care. She was a victim of child sexual exploitation, even then.'

'What?' I gasped. 'That is just not true. We moved because we wanted a fresh start. We hated the house in The Midlands and Bob was struggling for work. We moved to Blackpool because we thought it would be good for the children.'

The words sounded so hollow now but they were the truth. It was wicked to suggest that we were somehow running away from the authorities. And it was ridiculous too. If we were on the run, we would surely go a little further away.

'If social services wanted to take my daughter into care, they would have done so,' I snapped. 'I really don't think that moving house to Blackpool would put them off, it's hardly the other side of the world.'

The reporter raised his eyebrows a little and scribbled something in his notebook. I heard the stairs creaking and I realised Bob was on his way down.

The reporter said: 'We have information to suggest that Mr Downes brought home a succession of middle-aged men who stayed overnight, or even longer.

'And,' he paused, 'that Charlene was abused by some of these men.'

Bob appeared in the doorway, stared at him for a moment and then roared: 'Get out of my bloody house! Get out!'

The reporter seemed unruffled as he picked up his smart leather bag, brushed down his expensive suit as if dusting off invisible bugs and then left.

'The cheek of him!' I sobbed. 'How dare he?'

I had no idea where his information had come from, but it was wrong. Some of it was totally fabricated, some of it twisted. Certainly, Bob had friends round. He'd often have a mate round from the pub and occasionally they'd stay over on the couch if they'd had too much to drink. We didn't vet their backgrounds, I had never thought it was necessary – they were local blokes. Anyway, they had nothing to do with Charlene, or any of my children.

'He can't publish that,' Bob fumed.

But I remembered how the media had been during the trial – they had published outrageous slurs and had got away with it. What if it happened again? I just hoped this man had a conscience.

I pushed him to the back of my mind and continued planning the service. The night before, I decorated the church with pink roses, Charlene's favourite flowers. Placing a big photo of her in front of the altar, I choked back a sob. Even now, after ten long years, there were still moments when the shock of her disappearance left me reeling. It had never truly sunk in and I doubted it ever would.

The morning of the service, in November 2013, dawned grey and drizzly, but I had a firm sense of focus – I always felt nearer to Charlene on these sorts of occasions. And though I was heartbroken, I was determined to stay proud and strong. As I was getting ready my phone beeped with a text message from a friend who was attending the service with me later.

'Have you seen what they've written about Charlene?' she wrote. 'It's disgusting.'

I knew, instantly, it had to be the reporter from the week before. With my hair still damp, I dashed out to the newsagent's in my slippers. I flicked through the newsstand and then I felt sick inside. His newspaper – one of the posh ones who liked to look down their noses at me – had printed a story, suggesting Charlene had been nothing more than a prostitute. He also claimed that Bob and I were implicated in her disappearance. As I read, my blood ran cold. The article claimed that Charlene had made regular visits to a Salvation Army soup kitchen when she was just 11 years old, and a year later had been seen dancing outside a pub for men. It went on to say that, in the last few months of her short life, she had started swapping sexual favours with Arab and Asian takeaway workers. Three months before her disappearance, the article said that Charlene, along with another girl, had been driven by Asian men, to a lay-by in Blackburn. At midnight, she had gone off down an alley with one of the men and returned some time later. When she arrived back in Blackpool, she was given an envelope and told a friend: it was 'what I got for what I did in Blackburn'.

On another occasion, *The Times* claimed, Charlene had gone to Manchester in an old BMW, with a different Asian man. This had taken place less than a week before she disappeared. But neither incident was linked to the two men who stood trial over her murder.

And around a week before Charlene vanished, a white man with the 'motive and opportunity to murder Charlene' reportedly gave her £40, before meeting her again on that final evening. A police report had apparently described him as a 'compulsive, perverted paedophile' living in 'a squalid flat knee-deep in pornographic material of all types including those featuring young children'.

The article continued, saying that Lancashire Constabulary were today announcing a new investigation, pledging 'an open mind' about the murder. Its inquiry, said the article, would have no shortage of suspects, some were white; some were not.

It sounded as though the reporter was describing another girl entirely – Charlene had never come home after midnight. I had never been told – by the police or by anyone else – that she had been taken to Manchester and Blackburn by Asian men. And as for a white man with the motive to murder her? What did that mean? My mind boggled. How come he knew so much, and I didn't? As usual, I, as her mother, was the last to know. And it went on to say that Charlene was failed throughout her life and that up to this point, she had also been failed in death. It said that, according to reports, she was let down by everyone: her parents, care professionals and a police force that mismanaged a murder inquiry.

'let down by her parents'

My heart splintered and cracked. Nobody could blame me more than I blamed myself. I did feel that I had failed Charlene. I ought to have seen the signs, realised what was happening; I should have been able to save her. There is no greater pain for a mother than to know she has failed her child when she needed her the most. I had to live with that. But that didn't mean a faceless reporter from London was allowed to pull me apart too. On what grounds did he accuse me?

The last line of the article continued: 'Too little cared for, too little mourned.' It left me sobbing – rasping, choking sobs – right in the middle of the shop. Yes, I had my faults as a parent but nobody could say I didn't care. I missed and mourned Charlene every moment of my waking day – and in most of my dreams too. How could he possibly make such a cruel and crass statement?

He didn't know me. He didn't know Charlene. And he certainly didn't know our pain.

Charlene deserved better, just like the article said. Certainly, she deserved better from the British media. I was very rattled, and though I continued to get ready for the day, the words of that article swam around my head. How dare they? And on this, her special day, too. Was nothing sacred? I felt like a stray dog would have been given more consideration, more care, than my daughter. The media was fickle and shallow, I knew that, but this was beyond decent. This was Charlene's day and I refused to let anyone spoil it. I went to sit in her room, I cuddled her teddies and I buried my face in her pillow.

We had family and friends coming from all over the country. Marie McCourt, from SAMM, was attending too and had agreed to give a reading, Mum had friends who had travelled from Coventry. The girls and I owed it to everyone – to Charlene most of all – to be dignified. We got a taxi to the church, but as we pulled up, I spotted a BBC van. There were reporters and soundmen at the church gates. My heart sank.

'We'd like to talk to you about today's article,' shouted one. 'How do you feel?'

I was flabbergasted.

'This is my daughter's memorial service,' I said stiffly. 'Please show some respect.'

'We would really like your reaction,' he pressed. 'Don't you want to defend yourselves against the claims in the newspaper?'

I was torn. If I said nothing, did that make me look guilty?

'Maybe you should talk to them, Karen,' Mum said.

I nodded.

'Not here, not on the pavement,' I said.

Within minutes the reporters had found their way into the church vestry and they beckoned me inside. I was appalled – this seemed so disrespectful. The soundman shoved a long microphone into my face and I gulped.

'It's not true,' I gabbled. 'I'm so upset by it. This is Charlene's day … Please.'

By the time I made it into the church, the congregation was assembled and waiting. I took my place with Mum in one pew. Bob stood in another on the opposite side of the aisle. He knew there was something going on with me and we were barely speaking. Today, despite our shared pain, we couldn't reach out to each other. It was very sad. But then, I was used to being sad, it no longer really impacted me. The service was beautiful. Marie read the poem 'She is Gone' and Becki read a tribute which she had written herself.

'We will always miss you, Charlene,' Becki said sadly.

Next, Bob stood up to read.

'My little girl,' he said proudly, his voice choking with emotion. 'Your infectious smile filled the room. I know you're up there smiling, looking down on us as we cry. When it's my turn to go to heaven, I know you will be waiting at the gates, my darling daughter.'

Despite myself, I felt such a rush of love and empathy for him. There was a huge wedge between us, our marriage was a gaping, festering wound, but he was still her father. We all laid flowers on the altar. And afterwards, ten white doves were released, one for each year, in the churchyard.

'The service was beautiful, Mum,' Emma said, slipping her arm around me. 'Don't worry about the press, the people who matter are here today.'

She was right. I had found the service both heart-breaking and comforting. I wanted Charlene's name on everyone's lips, I wanted her to live on. Perversely, she would have loved to have been at her own memorial service – she loved church, singing and dancing. And she'd have given anything to let a dove go and watch it fly away, into the sky. It seemed so sad that she was missing it. Mum nodded her agreement.

'I miss her more each day,' she told me sadly.

* * *

The following day, the newspapers were filled with more horrific allegations.

A murdered schoolgirl who vanished ten years ago was sexually abused by as many as 100 men in the run-up to her death ... it emerged that police drew up a list of 100 'people of interest', suspected of abusing Charlene, including a succession of older white men.

'Enough!' I screeched, wringing my hands. 'Enough!'

Mum took a tissue and wiped her eyes; she didn't seem herself at all, she was quiet and a little distant. I wasn't sure whether it was the ten-year anniversary, or the vile newspaper articles which had affected her the most. But she seemed very frail and weary.

'I just don't have any energy,' she told me. 'I feel so old.'

We made a complaint to *The Times*. I spent hours writing a letter, but it was impossible to convey how hurt and angry and wronged I felt.

'You portrayed my daughter as a slut,' I wrote. 'She was just a little girl.'

Eventually, they wrote back. It was no surprise when they refused to apologise or retract their article. And so that was that – they knew full well that we couldn't afford to sue them. And of course that was why they were picking on us in the first place: we were uneducated, unsophisticated. And skint. We were the perfect target. Except, of course, that we were supposed to be the victims too.

One morning, later that month, I was in the kitchen, making Mum some toast and tea, to surprise her with breakfast in bed. Then Bob shouted and I could hear, from his voice, that it was urgent.

'Karen!' he called. 'It's your mum!'

I hurried into Mum's room and found her sitting on the edge of her bed, unsteadily clutching his hand.

'Jessie's not well,' he said anxiously.

Mum was doubled over, grey with pain. I didn't like the look of her one bit and so I called an ambulance immediately.

'Your mum's getting on in years,' the doctor said. 'She has lots of complications arising from diabetes.'

'But she'll be OK, won't she?' I asked anxiously. 'She's a tough old boot. She's been through a lot, she can get through this.'

I was talking myself into believing it, I knew that.

I spent the afternoon with her and promised to come back that evening.

'I'll fetch a new nightie for you and your slippers,' I promised.

'Bring me a photo of Charlene,' she said feebly. 'The one by my bed.'

On my way home, I popped in to tell Mark that I couldn't meet him that night, as we'd planned.

'I have to visit Mum, she's in hospital,' I told him.

But his reaction was bizarre.

'You're not going anywhere without me,' he told me viciously. 'Forget about your mum, you're seeing me tonight.'

I was aghast.

'She's an old lady and she needs me,' I insisted.

'Oh, she should be in a home,' he retorted. 'I don't know why you're bothering with her.'

Annoyed with myself for even calling in to see him in the first place, I grabbed my bag. Soon, I was out on the street, on my way home, with Mark marching furiously alongside.

'Leave me alone!' I snapped. 'I can't believe the way you spoke about my poor mum. Just leave me alone!'

Suddenly, he lunged at me and pulled at my hair. He grabbed my bun and yanked my head backwards with such force, I felt a pain shoot through my neck. I screamed at the top of my voice. A passing car stopped and called to me, but Mark dragged me off down the street.

'I'll call the police,' yelled the driver.

Further down the road, a police car stopped and an officer jumped out. I was amazed at how quickly they had managed to get there. I was filled with gratitude for the car driver; I didn't even know his name. Mark was arrested and hauled off into the waiting police car. Dazed, I tried to gather my composure. I had to go to the station and make a statement, with my bruises stinging, clothes bedraggled, and make-up smudged across my cheeks.

'This will go to court,' the officers told me.

I felt so ashamed – as though it was my fault somehow. Surely I was old enough to know better by now? I had got myself involved in such a mess. I knew I'd have to tell Bob too – he'd be sure to find out. And as with all our family's dirty linen, the incident was soon reported in the local paper. 'Besotted Kiwi Attacked Mum Of Missing Girl!' the headline screamed.

Bob was angry, and had every right to be.

'Don't you think we've been through enough without this?' he shouted, waving the newspaper in my face. 'The whole bloody town is laughing at you. And me!'

But I told him our marriage was over, and had been for a long time.

In December 2013, Mark admitted assault and was ordered to stay away from me. I still cared for him, I had to admit – it was impossible to switch off my emotions – but I was relieved too that our relationship was over. He had become too intense, too controlling. But Mark didn't seem to care what the courts said: he called and texted me all the time. He was relentless; wheedling his way back in, laying on the charm one minute, guilt the next.

'I spent my life savings to come and be with you,' he whined. 'I left my poor mum, my entire life behind – all for you. I've no money to go back home and you're all I have here.'

Gradually, he wore me down. I began to feel responsible, as though I at least owed him this.

'One final chance,' I agreed.

But we had only been back together for a few days and he was already whining at me to leave Bob.

* * *

I visited the hospital every day. Sometimes, I'd find Mum clutching her photo of Charlene and praying. But she was deteriorating. The doctors warned her heart was very weak. Then Christmas 2013 came, with the announcement I had been dreading: there was nothing more they could do to help her.

'She has heart failure,' one of the medical team told me. 'She won't last much longer, I'm sorry.'

'I want to bring her home,' I said. 'I'll look after her.'

I knew, without even asking, that Bob would agree. We got a hospital bed in the front room for her; Bob moved the sofa out of the way to make room. She came home by ambulance and Bob, Becki, Emma and I were all there to greet her: her last homecoming. Looking into her eyes, tired and beaten, she knew it too. She had to have a wheelchair just for those few steps from the pavement outside into our living room, she had become so weak. And for those last two months, I hardly left her side. She had oxygen from our local hospice and carers came in four times a day to help, but I helped to wash and dress and feed her.

Bob was wonderful too, taking turns to sit with her, as the end drew near. Sometimes, she would slip down, on her pillows, and I wasn't strong enough to lift her back up and make her comfy again. But he would always help – it didn't matter what time of the day or night it was.

'There we go, Jessie.' He smiled. 'All better now.'

He was as tender and gentle as any nurse. I appreciated his support, during those darkest of days, and I wished we hadn't got to the stage where I could no longer tell him so. Towards the end, Mum became confused and she didn't make much sense sometimes. But in a very clear voice, she said to me: 'I will look after Charlene, for you, Karen. Don't worry about her, I will be there.'

Her words comforted and chilled me, all at once. I felt certain she was having some sort of vision – a tantalising glimpse of what was to come. For though death was the final terror, for me, it also held such promise and allure. Because in death – and perhaps only then – I would see my daughter again. Hours later, I held Mum's hand, now clammy and cold, as she took her last, shallow breath. She was 78 years old. Sobbing on her chest, I felt totally lost – Mum had always been there for me, always. And I knew deep down that losing Charlene had killed her: she had died of a broken heart.

Her funeral, in February 2014, was booked at Carleton Crematorium – Charlene's bench was there, and so it seemed the perfect place. Mark insisted on meeting me, in the morning, before the service.

'I want to come to the funeral,' he insisted.

'No,' I said. 'I'm sorry, it will cause too much trouble.'

I stood my ground, for Mum's sake. But Mark was furious. My stomach was churning as I left his flat, worried about what he might do next.

Somehow, we managed to get through the service and say our goodbyes. It was a small, private service, attended by those who loved her the most. And with this in mind, I took Charlene's photo in my bag; I had put photos in Mum's coffin too.

'She's here with us, Mum,' I whispered. 'She's here for you.'

We had the hymn 'O Love That Wilt Not Let Me Go' – we had sung it at the recent memorial service too. And the same vicar had agreed to take charge of Mum's funeral.

'She would like that.' I nodded. 'They both would.'

At the service I gave a eulogy.

'She was there every single day of my life,' I said proudly. 'From being a little girl, she was both mum and dad for me, and she did the most wonderful job. She was a loving and amazing grandmother to my children.

'And since Charlene went missing, she has, quite literally, kept me alive.'

Bob and I were polite to one another all day but he didn't come in the funeral car with me and the girls, he followed on separately in a taxi. It was almost as if he wasn't part of the family any more. Mum was cremated, and afterwards I kept her ashes at home with me – it was what she would have wanted, her family meant everything to her.

* * *

Days after the funeral, Mark was still simmering. I was walking on eggshells, trying to keep him happy, knowing the slightest little slip could set him off. One morning, a month on, I got a text from him, asking me to meet him in a car park, near the flat he was renting. He wanted food and money from me, and asked if we could move in together, to start saving.

'Not this again, Mark!' I sighed. 'You know I have to think about my family. I've just lost my mum, I'm just not ready.'

At the thought of Mum my eyes welled with tears. I started to walk away, but he followed. From behind, he grabbed my hair and pulled me backwards, sharply.

'When are you going to move out?' he yelled. 'You bitch!'

I screamed in pain.

'Stop it!' I begged.

From across the road, I heard a man shout: 'Karen!' and an old friend luckily came dashing over to me. He pulled Mark away and rang for the police. I stumbled and fell into a heap on the ground, retching and sobbing. My knees were bleeding and my head was pounding. I heard sirens and two officers jumped out of a car and ran to arrest Mark. He was gasping, breathless, bent double as though in shock, his anger suddenly dissolved. I had to make another statement, and my friend did too. It was becoming a poisonous cycle – and I was stuck in the middle of it; I didn't know how to get out. Normally, this was where I'd have turned to Mum for advice.

What I wouldn't give for a brew and a natter right now, I told myself sadly. *I miss you so much, Mum.*

In March 2014, Mark pleaded guilty to assault before Blackpool Magistrates' Court and was given a six-month supervision order and a six-month restraining order. Of course the local paper pounced on the story – the next juicy chapter of my car-crash life.

Straight after the assault, I had told Mark it was over, once and for all.

'But I love you,' he bleated.

'I mean it.'

For a couple of months, he left me alone and I began to believe he had moved on with his life. But then, the calls and the text messages started. But I didn't reply, I knew I had to be strong. Then, one night, I heard stones hitting the bedroom window outside.

Mark was persistent. He shouted louder and louder, and when I heard Bob growling on the stairs, my heart sank.

'Please, Bob,' I pleaded, 'don't make it worse.'

But Bob marched outside and shouted: 'Get away, you bloody lunatic!'

From the window, I watched, half-fascinated, half-horrified, as Bob chased him down the street, arms waving, insults flying. I didn't want to call the police. I couldn't bear to bring any more trouble to our door. But Mark continued to text and call me and come to the house. One night, Emma was visiting, and she chased him down the street with a volley of insults.

'Don't come anywhere near my mum again!' she warned. 'Or else!'

But he didn't listen. And eventually, I gave in. It wasn't a conscious decision – it was more the fact that I didn't have the strength to stand up to him. Losing Mum had hit me so hard and I was swamped with grief – I didn't feel I could cope with anything else. Not just now. I felt embarrassed too, that I had let it get this far. I felt too ashamed to tell my family that I was scared of Mark, that he was controlling me and humiliating me. Besides, I had started the affair – I had chosen him – and now I had to suffer the consequences. It had been a bit of fun, a moment of madness, but it had mutated into something so ugly and toxic that I couldn't see a way out.

You made your bed, you lie in it, Karen, I told myself harshly.

I also longed for that feeling again, of the freedom and happiness of our early relationship. Mark had given me that once – why not again? Why couldn't we rewind to the good times? And so, the relationship went on, and day by day my self-esteem was chipped away. I was miserable, lost in grief and loneliness.

One day, Mark called me wanting money. I felt guilty, as though it was my fault he didn't have any. These days, everything seemed to be my fault; I didn't have any confidence left in myself to think any different. So I hurried over to his bedsit, with some cash, biting my lip and worrying, all the way there. But the moment I arrived, he snatched it from me.

'I want you back here tonight,' he snapped.

'Oh, I can't, Mark,' I said apologetically. 'Becki is coming to see me this afternoon. I'm taking my family out, it's all arranged.'

'You're putting that stupid bitch before me!' he snarled. 'I don't want you seeing your kids, I've told you this before.'

He grabbed something from a drawer behind him. I spotted the glint of a blade and to my horror, I saw it was a white-handled kitchen knife.

'Mark!' I protested. 'What are you doing?'

He raised the knife to my face, his face bloated, breath putrid, and hissed: 'You're going to stay tonight, aren't you? You know what will happen if you don't. I'll chop you up, I'll kill that family of yours as well.'

My teeth were chattering so loudly, I felt the vibrations right through my body. I was terrified. And in that moment of sheer panic, I thought of Charlene: how frightened she must have been, how sad and lonely, in those final moments. The point of the knife was digging at my throat now. Mark's face was inches from mine, his eyes popping, spittle flying from his lips. He looked like a madman. Facing the very real possibility that I was going to die, I closed my eyes and saw a vivid image of Charlene, reaching out, pleading for help.

'Mummy,' she whispered softly.

Her eyes were shining with tears and pain, her voice so faint and fragile that I could barely hear her.

'I can't find you,' I sobbed. 'I'm trying, darling. I'll keep trying.'

Then, with a jolt, my eyes snapped back open. The TV was blaring full blast. Like a man possessed, Mark was turning up the sound and pulling down the blinds. I realised he was trying to drown out my screams. And I just wanted it to be over. With a vicious tug, he yanked my hair back and punched me twice in the face. Then, he pressed the knife against my leg and shouted: 'You will come back tomorrow or you know what will happen. You will do what I say, when I say.'

My survival instinct kicked in. I tried to fight back but he was younger and stronger than me. He slapped me hard across the face, leaving my ears ringing, and pressed the knife to my throat once again.

Thinking at a million miles an hour, my mind whirring, I managed to say: 'Mark, I will come back later. You know I will. I love you.'

On the street outside, I looked around wildly for the nearest phone box and rang the police.

'Help!' I screamed. 'Help me!'

I was bloody and bruised; shocked and stunned, but grateful to be alive. Mark was arrested soon after, climbing out of a window in his flat. One officer needed a taser to subdue him. I had to make a statement and he appeared in court in October 2015 and admitted affray. This time I knew things had gone too far: he was dominating me, ruining me. I had made a dreadful mistake. I couldn't bear to tell the children – they had no idea that I had even gone back to Mark this time. I hadn't wanted to worry them, I knew they'd be dreadfully disappointed.

Maybe I can keep it quiet somehow, I thought.

But the case made the front page of the *Blackpool Gazette* and I was mortified.

'Mum, why didn't you tell us?' Robert raged. 'I'll kill him if he touches you again.'

Bob bought a copy of the newspaper and we sat in silence as he read the report. But instead of exploding, he folded the newspaper and sighed.

'Karen, you really need to take control of your life back,' he told me. 'I am worried about you. Do what you like, but don't put yourself at risk.'

His sympathy really hurt. I was reminded of the day Charlene had disappeared. When Bob was kind to me, I knew things were bad; I wished he'd scream and shout instead. I felt stupid, ashamed and guilty, but I knew he was right. And that night I heard Mum whispering my name.

'Come on, Karen,' she said gently. 'Put the kettle on and have a Rich Tea biscuit. You don't need an idiot like Mark Bailey.'

I cried and ached with exhaustion. It was over. I missed him, or perhaps I missed the idea of him – I missed the destructive habit that he had become. But I knew, with total certainty, that I would never go back.

Mark remained in the UK and settled just a few miles away from me. I hoped he might find a new partner but really, I didn't want to know. And I was fortunate that I didn't see him very often. Occasionally, in the supermarket, or perhaps across the street, I'd spot him skulking by. But I never even made eye contact.

Bob and I limped on, just as before, almost as if nothing had happened. Part of me wanted him to demand some sort of showdown: I wanted crisis talks and tears and passion, I wanted to know that he cared. But I also knew that Bob never was, and never would be, that sort of man. He didn't refer to the elephants in the room. Skeletons in the drawer. We had a whole collection in our family. And maybe, I was partly to blame.

Despite everything, I couldn't bring myself to leave him. He and I were bound together. We loved and missed our daughter in equal measure and there was no way out of that. He was the only person who came close to knowing the pain I carried with me; I just couldn't let that go. There was something intangible, something stronger even than a marriage vow, that kept us together.

I began grieving, quietly, for Mum. I spent hours at Charlene's bench, thinking of them both, wondering if they were together. My heart ached to see them. And yet it was some comfort to know that they might be looking after each other, singing, dancing and telling stories, in twin beds, side by side, in heaven.

CHAPTER TWENTY-SEVEN
THE WORLD LISTENS AT LAST

In 2014, just before the anniversary of Charlene's disappearance, Becki called me to say she'd had journalists from BBC's *Panorama* knocking on her door, asking for an interview.

'Will you speak to them, Mum?' she asked. 'We could do it together.'

'It's been 11 years,' I told the cameras. 'My family needs closure.'

Soon after, I was contacted by BBC's *Crimewatch*, who also said they wanted to make a programme about Charlene.

'We'd like you and your family to take part,' the researcher told me.

I wanted to do it – I knew a huge audience would be so useful. Somebody knew what had happened to Charlene. Someone knew where her body was. And we needed that person to come forward. Becki agreed to speak too. Emma was too shy, and she grieved in her own way and stayed well away from the press, but I understood that. Bob and Robert kept their feelings private too.

On Bonfire Night 2014, Becki and I went to the Hilton Hotel, on the promenade, to be filmed. On the way there, I could smell smoke and cordite and there was an explosion of colour and sparkle in the sky; I wondered if Charlene could see it too. In the hotel lobby, there were two actresses, who would play the roles of Charlene and me in the reconstruction. It was odd, unsettling, freaky even. But I was used to these feelings by now. I'd had the sensation, quite often over the years, that I was looking in on my own life. That events were so bizarre or so heartbreaking that they couldn't actually be happening to me. And here it was, the living proof – it was happening to someone else after all. But seeing them walk off so jauntily, in the direction of the prom, tore at my heart. That was just how it had once been. And so, where was she now?

But it wasn't lost on me, not one bit, that Charlene would actually have loved all this – the cameras, the make-up artists, the fancy hotel. Someone brought us one of those posh frothy coffees with a single biscuit in a wrapper on the saucer. I could just imagine Charlene's face as she scooped out the froth. She'd have had so much fun – and it was all in her honour.

'You're not here to see it, Babby,' I whispered sadly.

The following week, we settled down, as a family, to watch *The Girl Who Vanished*. My eyes swam with tears as a photo of Charlene came on the screen. Becki's interview, and mine, were played. And then, to my horror, one of the defendants from the trial, Mohammed Raveshi, appeared on the TV.

'They interviewed him!' Bob raged. '*Him*! Why didn't you tell me you were appearing on the same programme as him?'

He stormed out of the room. I could hardly blame him – my own blood was boiling too. I felt as though I'd been tricked into taking part in the documentary. I wanted my message out there, I wanted Charlene's name to live on, yet this was an awful, impossible bargain to make. As Raveshi spoke, I found myself slammed right back at the trial. In my mind, I was in court, rigid with fear, listening to those evil tapes.

'Switch it off!' Bob shouted, marching back into the living room. 'I won't have his face in my house.'

'Leave it on!' I demanded. 'This is for Charlene.'

It was ridiculous – Bob and I were shouting so loudly, we couldn't even hear the TV. Somehow I managed to calm myself down and concentrate on the rest of the programme. Even as her mother, right at the centre of it, I had to admit that the statistics in the case were mind-blowing, especially when you considered that we still had no answers. The investigation had become the largest-ever missing person inquiry undertaken by Lancashire Police, with more than 4,800 witness statements. They had followed 10,500 lines of inquiry. A specialist missing persons bureau had generated a picture of Charlene as they thought she might look now, as a young woman. The image, when it flashed onto the screen, almost made my heart stop.

'It's Charlene, and yet it isn't!' I gasped.

The image reminded me more of myself than of her. It gave me an uncomfortable feeling – and yet a great sense of yearning too.

The following month, the *Crimewatch* programme aired. Now, the police were offering a reward of £100,000.

'Too little, too late,' I said.

Our interviews played. The reconstruction film took my breath away. There I was again, standing on the outside, looking in at my own life. *My old life*. And wishing I could have it back once again. Afterwards, I had a phone call from a man named Eric Shelmerdine, General Secretary of The Association of British Investigators. He explained that they wanted to help.

'The case doesn't have the same profile as Madeleine McCann,' he said. 'We'd like to change that.'

He explained that the ABI is the home of professional private sector investigation in the UK, and he offered to put Charlene's story on their website. He promised that their 400 investigators would begin working to solve the mystery of her disappearance. I was so grateful.

'Bless you,' I said, gulping back tears.

* * *

Suddenly, everyone was talking about Charlene. I had so many offers of support, so many promises of help, but I couldn't – wouldn't – ever forget those first few months after my daughter disappeared when nobody wanted to even print her name. But it was more publicity for Charlene, and I was grateful for every drop. I didn't care who I worked with, what politics they were peddling, what agenda they had, I just wanted justice for my daughter. If I couldn't have her home, then I wanted the truth of what had happened – as her mother, I needed to know.

In April 2015, the family of the missing girl, Paige Chivers, finally got justice. Robert Ewing, 60, was found guilty of her murder and of perverting the course of justice. The court was told how Ewing had carefully groomed Paige and had taken an 'inappropriate sexual interest' in her. Gareth Dewhurst, 46, was convicted of helping him dispose of her body and also of perverting the course of justice. A shiver ran down my spine as I read the court reports, day after day. The similarities to Charlene's story were as startling as they were tragic. Despite extensive searches, Paige's body had never been found. Paige, 15, had gone missing on 23rd August 2007, after a row on the phone with her father, Frank, about missing cash. The family had struggled to cope and their home life had become chaotic after Paige's mother had died in February 2007 from a heart attack.

Just like Charlene, going off the rails, with nobody there to save her, I thought sadly.

Frank Chivers had reported his daughter missing three days later, but the police had botched their initial response. Preston Crown Court heard him clearly state she was 15, but her date of birth was wrongly entered on the police system as 1962 and not 1992. As a result, the matter was dealt with as though Paige were an adult, aged 45, who had moved on voluntarily, rather than a girl of 15, who was missing from home. It was not corrected until 7th September 2007 and vital hours in the search were missed. After the court case, a police spokesman said: 'We fully recognise and accept that an error was made when Paige was first reported missing. Quite simply, her year of birth was recorded as 1962 and not 1992. While our focus quite rightly up to this juncture has been on the criminal investigation, this matter will now be voluntarily referred to the Independent Police Complaints Commission.'

I threw the newspaper down in disgust.

'What good is that?' I demanded, shouting at an empty living room. 'An investigation into her death won't help anyone. It's just like Charlene, all over again. All over again.'

I felt so frustrated that lessons were not being learned. And for Paige's father, Frank, any investigation was totally pointless. I had watched him, heartbroken, laying flowers on the promenade on the anniversaries of her disappearance. Grieving for both his wife and daughter, he had fallen into drug use and was found collapsed outside his flat, in August 2013, with a bleed on the brain. He had been kicked in the head following a petty argument over a £20 note with a known drug dealer. Sean Conlon was jailed for life in February 2014 at Preston Crown Court. Paige's father had died without seeing justice done. And I feared, with the weight of my burden, the very same thing might happen to me.

CHAPTER TWENTY-EIGHT
THE FOOTAGE

It was a chilly day in October 2016 and I was feeling down and despondent with another anniversary approaching. We were no further on than we had been 13 years earlier.

I got a call from Detective Inspector Andrew Webster, the latest officer working on the case. He had also been the officer working on the Paige Chivers case. In the past, a call from the police would have sent my heart racing. A sighting? An arrest? A breakthrough? But I no longer felt any kind of anticipation when I heard his voice – I had learned my lesson in the hardest of ways.

'Can you come down to the station with Bob?' he asked. 'There's something we'd like to show you.'

There was no sense of excitement or expectancy. I lay awake, as I did every night, thinking about my daughter. But I wasn't banking on anything new. However, as Bob and I sat down the following day, in an interview room, DI Webster flicked open a laptop and cleared his throat.

'We've found some footage of Charlene from the day she disappeared,' he said.

I stared at him, stunned. Bob gulped audibly.

'Where has it been, all these years?' I spluttered.

'It was in the archive,' he replied lamely.

The police had assured me, back in 2003, that they had checked every camera and watched all the CCTV they could find. And now – a staggering 13 years on – it had suddenly popped up, from nowhere.

My mind was reeling. It beggared belief. But before I could speak again, the footage started to play, and my heart lurched. I'd had no idea what was in store.

'That's her!' I gasped, tears streaming down my cheeks. 'I recognise her clothes, the way she's walking.'

Charlene had on her black jeans and her patterned jumper. She was walking casually past Price Buster: innocent, carefree, *alive*. Was she giggling? I could almost swear it, but the footage was a little too grainy to be sure. It took me right back to the day she had vanished – the day our lives fell to pieces. Instinctively, I put my arms out to her – I wanted to reach out into the film and bring her back home. Like a little child, I wanted to run around the back of the screen to find her and pluck her out.

'I'm here, Charlene,' I sobbed. 'Mummy is here! Come home.'

Eight seconds later, it was over. Eight seconds of pure agony and ecstasy. Of comfort and torture. Of life – and an end to it. Though it tore me apart, I felt myself wanting to watch the footage over and over again. I felt so close to my daughter – so close I could touch her. Bob was in shock, he didn't speak. But, as I wiped away my tears, I felt my frustration bubbling.

'This footage would have been so useful, 13 years ago,' I said sharply. 'Why has this taken so long?'

But the detective didn't apologise.

'This is a step forward,' he insisted. 'It might be very useful. We're hoping for a big response from the public.'

The footage was released online, on the anniversary of Charlene's disappearance. It appeared in every newspaper and on every news channel. DI Webster released a statement, too, and I heard it played over and over, on radios and TVs and mobile phones: 'We're determined to find out what happened to Charlene and part of that is trying to trace her last movements.

'She was last seen at around 10:30pm on 1st November 2003, in an alleyway just off Abingdon Street. We want to identify people who lived and worked in that area.

'We have established she was sexually exploited. We would like to speak to other victims of sexual exploitation around that time. They may hold bits of information that may help us to take this forward.'

In her own little way, Charlene would have loved this. *She is famous*, I thought wryly. *She even has her own Wikipedia page now.*

'Google me!' she would say, laughing hysterically.

But what a ransom she had paid. What a price. Emma and Becki came round. They broke down when they viewed the footage. Emma watched it only twice, and Robert saw it once on a later occasion, before flicking it off angrily.

'I don't want to see it,' he said. 'I can't.'

For Becki, more than anyone, it was heartbreaking.

'It's freaking me out, Mum,' she told me. 'I'm right back there, on that day. I should have looked after her, I should have made her come home.'

The CCTV footage had sent us all crashing back to 1st November 2003 and it made me realise that in the intervening years we had, without realising, moved on a little with our grief. Now, we were slipping helplessly backwards once again and it was almost too painful to bear. The footage was not exactly therapeutic, yet it was strangely addictive. If the police were correct – that Charlene was killed hours after her disappearance – then this was footage of my daughter walking to her death. It was hardly a family heirloom but I became obsessed. I couldn't stop playing it – switching it off was like letting Charlene go. I reminded myself of Charlene, with her Darren Day DVD, pressing rewind and play, rewind and play, over and over again. Like me, she wanted the moment to last forever.

'Switch that flipping song off!' I had said to her. 'I am sick of listening to Darren Day. Honestly, Charlene!'

And now, I was doing the exact same thing; I was caught in the trap.

'You have to stop playing it,' Becki ordered. 'I know why you're doing it, but this is no good for you, Mum.'

She was right. But it was so hard. I had to wean myself away from it, distance myself, and accept it held nothing more than a memory, an empty promise. Worst of all, when I called DI Webster, a month after the anniversary, he said there were no new leads, no new witnesses from the CCTV.

Nobody came forward.

'It's too late,' I said bitterly. 'People have moved on, our chance has gone.'

Yet another knockout blow. And I wasn't sure how many times I could keep on staggering to my feet and coming back for more. But in August 2017, DI Webster contacted me once again.

'We'd like to see you,' he announced.

'Here we go again,' I said wearily. 'Here we go again.'

That I had become almost glib and sarcastic when the police called was a reflection of how low I had sunk. Despite the call, or maybe because of it, I felt flat and depressed. Bob and I went along, as instructed. It was like being summoned to see a failing headmaster who'd lost the respect of the school kids long ago.

'What now?' I asked impatiently. 'What is it?'

'We've made an arrest, in connection with Charlene's murder,' said Webster. 'We don't want you to get your hopes up.'

My jaw dropped. This was the last thing I'd expected. I felt my heart begin to race.

'Who?' I stammered. 'When? Do we know him?'

I was totally bewildered. This was a completely new line of inquiry. The man arrested was a convicted paedophile, who was currently serving time in prison for indecently assaulting two girls. I racked my brains.

'Come on, Karen. Think!'

The name meant nothing to me. DI Webster said there was nothing to suggest I would ever have set eyes on him. I walked out of the police station in a trance, with Bob trailing behind, not sure how I was supposed to feel. But even though I had vowed not to get my hopes up, it was impossible. Deep down, I still had faith. The tiniest part of me still held out a glimmer of hope that Charlene might be alive. But I never voiced that. For self-preservation, I had learned to bury any optimism I might feel although it was still there, the embers flickering, glowing in my soul. Overnight, at home, I was on tenterhooks, waiting for a phone call. I didn't sleep, I couldn't eat. Morning came and I was wide awake, psyched up, my nerves shredded.

It was late in the day when police finally sent a car, and Bob and I went off to the police station again – as confused and agitated as we were hopeful. DI Webster took a seat opposite us and I tried desperately to read the emotions in his face, to second-guess what he was about to say.

'We've let the suspect go. No charges, I'm afraid,' he said. 'I'm sorry, I really am. It goes on.'

And on. *And on.* I wept; Bob wept. He reached his arms out to me and we held each other. Our first cuddle for years. It wasn't as though we hadn't experienced this before but that didn't make it any less heart-rending. The car drove us home, dropped us off and we went inside. To wait.

'It's a lot to take in,' said Bob. 'It's a lot to cope with.'

And it certainly was. I realised that, when you stripped away the police, the courts, the media, the politicians, the cranks, the do-gooders – the do-*badders*, the whole crazy circus that our daughter's disappearance had become – it was just me and Bob. Just as it had been, before this all started. She was our daughter. *Our girl.* We couldn't count on anyone else. And with that, I pulled him in a little closer.

EPILOGUE

Although it was only September 2017, there was a nip of autumn in the air and I flicked on the heating guiltily, knowing Bob would disapprove. Sure enough, he came into the living room soon after, felt the radiator and grunted.

'You could put a jumper on instead,' he admonished, laughing despite himself.

We were both excited and nothing could dampen the mood. Emma was bringing her three children, Riley, Ethan and baby Tallulah, to stay for the weekend and we had so much planned. She lived with her partner, Pete, in Preston, about a 20-minute drive away from us. I was like a kid myself as I ran through the schedule in my head. The births of my grandchildren, six in total, had brought me a new-found serenity and a sense of peace that I would never have thought possible.

Charlene is still a part of our daily lives; she is there in every thought. Every tear. Every smile. But it is almost

14 years on, and I am learning to remember her with love and warmth. And my precious grandchildren, though they don't know it, have been my therapists. Each new life, in turn, has been a stepping stone to a brighter place. There are days when, in surprise, I hear myself laughing. And it is all thanks to them. I will never 'get over' losing Charlene, that is unthinkable. There is no forgiveness for her killers, whoever and wherever they are. The case is always open, of course. The police say they will never give up. But I have reached a sense of acceptance and calm.

Emma's eldest, Riley, is now seven years old. I had been to all the scans and antenatal appointments and I was thrilled when he was born. Holding him in my arms, in the maternity unit, I felt the tiniest piece of my broken heart healing.

'He's truly beautiful,' I told her.

'Charlene would love him,' Emma agreed.

There was an undeniable sadness. Every happy occasion was a bittersweet moment, it always would be. But it was nonetheless impossible to be in low spirits with a new baby in the family. Just the feel of his baby-soft skin against my cheek gave me such a feeling of contentment. And the purity and innocence only a baby can bring gradually began to wash away the stains and ground-in anguish left by the court case. Riley was a godsend, a little miracle. Emma's second son, Ethan, arrived on December

10 2013. And because Pete was so squeamish, I was given the honour of being her birthing partner.

'Are you sure?' I whooped. 'I can't wait!'

I had never been a birthing partner before. For weeks beforehand, I was on red alert, my hospital bag packed. I refused to go too far from the house, I hardly even slept.

'Anyone would think you were the one having the baby!' Emma teased.

I was more than ready. When the call came, it was at 6am. In the stillness of the early morning, I heard a faint giggle, and I could have sworn I felt a light touch on my cheek. I knew it was Charlene, watching over us, wherever she was. This was a big day for our family, and she wanted to share it.

'Look after your sister today, Charlene,' I whispered.

I called a cab and raced to hospital, panting for breath by the time I reached the labour ward. Emma was already inside. I mopped her forehead and held her hand as she bravely gritted her teeth through the pain. Little Ethan was born at 3:30 that afternoon. I cut his cord and helped to dress him. I had bought him a cute little hat, saying: 'Welcome to the World'.

'I'm going to give him "Charlie" as a middle name, after his aunty,' Emma told me. 'I'll christen him on Charlene's birthday.'

I sobbed with emotion. They shared a name and a lifelong link – this little boy was most definitely sent by her, I felt sure of it. It was less than two months after Ethan's birth that Mum passed away and the family was shattered, lost without our figurehead. But little Ethan kept us all going. Watching his new life unfold was the perfect antidote to the emptiness and pain of grief. The following March, on what would have been Charlene's 25th birthday, Ethan was christened at The Central Methodist Church in Blackpool. I wore a pink top and black trousers, and in my handbag I carried a little photo of Charlene. Her photos was there in church too, on the altar – a reminder that she was with us. And because Ethan shared his special christening day with his Aunty Charlene's birthday, we now had a reason to smile again and to celebrate the day every year.

Two years on, and Emma was pregnant again. And this time, a scan showed that she was carrying a little girl. The pregnancy went well, but she and Pete and their young family decided to move away from Blackpool.

'I couldn't bring a daughter up in Blackpool,' she told me. 'Not after what happened.'

I nodded; I understood. Besides, she was only a short drive away and I still saw a lot of her and the children. The plan was for me to be her birthing partner again.

'I'd love to,' I told her. 'I really would.'

But during the night, three weeks before her due date, Emma fell ill and had to be rushed to hospital. She was diagnosed with septicaemia and her life hung in the balance. Little Tallulah Charlene, named again after her aunt, was born soon after, on June 6 2017, weighing 6lb 13oz. Poor Pete was so distraught, and it all happened so fast, he didn't call me until after the drama was over. By the time I heard, early the following morning, both mum and baby were thankfully out of danger. I went straight to the hospital and Tallulah was truly beautiful. She looked so much like her mummy, and a little like Charlene too.

'She lives on, through Tallulah,' I said.

Robert has sadly split with his partner but he has three lovely children himself: Ashton, Maisie and Rori. The children know all about Charlene. They went to her bench, took flowers and had their photos taken there. Maisie reminds me of Charlene more than any of my grandchildren. She is only five years old, but has the outlook of a little old lady. I know my mum would have adored her – the two of them would have been best pals, just as she and Charlene were.

'I saw Aunty Char-Char by my bed, Nanna,' she told me. 'She tickles me sometimes and makes me laugh when I'm supposed to be asleep.'

'She's with the angels now,' I told Maisie.

'I know that,' she answered stroppily. 'Course I know that, Nanna. But she can still be my Aunty Char-Char!'

I smiled. Charlene was almost an imaginary friend for her. Of course the two of them had never met. Would *never* meet, I had to accept that now, yet there was a beautiful bond between them. And then, Becki announced that she was pregnant with a son. She was single and so it wasn't easy for her. But she was pleased, all the same.

'I'm going to give my baby "Charlie" as the middle name,' she told me proudly. 'We'll never forget her, Mum. *Never.*'

* * *

As I finished pumping up the airbeds, ready for my grand-children's arrival, I heard the back door being flung open and there was a rush of excited chatter and giggling.

'Donkeys, Granda!' they shouted. 'Donkeys!'

From the sounds of it, they had thrown themselves onto Bob and he was laughing even louder than they were. That was good to hear, too. Bob hadn't laughed for many years after Charlene disappeared. He had suffered; he had sobbed. He'd lost himself somewhere along the way, just as I had. And yet, despite our trou-bles – and God knows we'd had an overflowing bucket full of them – we were still together. Yes, we were bound by the tragedy of the past, but glued together by our future – our children and our grandchildren, and our hopes and dreams for them.

'Hang on, I'm coming for a donkey ride too!' I called, taking the stairs two at a time.

Ethan threw his arms around me.

'Nanna, I love you!' he declared dramatically.

The earnest expression on his little face made me want to laugh and cry all at once. Coats on, buttoned up against the chill, we walked along to the furthest part of the beach to find the donkeys. The children stuffed stones and shells in their pockets and when theirs were full, they borrowed mine. It brought back happy memories.

'I don't want dirty stones in my pockets!' I protested, but the kids just laughed.

We didn't go on the pier, we avoided the slot machines and the takeaways. Some things were, and always would be, too raw. The pier loomed like a large bogeyman on the horizon. We scurried past; I felt the children could be somehow tainted or sucked in if we went too close. On the way home, the Illuminations began to flicker on and the children's faces lit up in wonder and amazement, just as Charlene's had. I could almost hear her faint laughter, carrying on the wind as it blew off the sea.

Bob said: 'Who fancies fish and chips for tea?' and the kids screamed their approval.

Sitting around the table, the smell of vinegar stinging my nose, we looked towards Charlene's photo on the fireplace. As always, we said a short prayer for her before we ate.

'Hello, Aunty Cha-Cha,' said Riley.

'She loves you all,' I told them fondly.

* * *

It gives me so much comfort that Charlene lives on in their hearts. Each birthday, we buy her a cake and sing to her. At Christmas, I light candles and I buy pink roses, her favourite. I have bought cards for every occasion and I've kept every single one, in a box, in my bedroom. On the anniversary of her disappearance, we gather at her memorial bench and remember her with smiles.

'Remember how she stole my dolls,' Becki says. 'She didn't even like dolls, she just loved to cause a fuss.'

'Or the time we waited two hours in the rain for Darren Day to come out of the stage door?' I laugh.

We have so many memories. We've had 14 years without her, but we also had 14 wonderful years with her, and I will always be grateful for that time with my daughter. Sometimes, on days when I'm feeling strong enough, I walk past our old family home. And on occasion, just as the light is fading, I have seen Charlene's face, peering out of the top window. Her bedroom was at the front of the house and I fancy I can see her – the suggestion of her spirit, a dancing shadow of herself – waving happily at me.

'Mummy!' she shouts. 'I'm here. I'm home, Mummy! I'm here.'

Those three words were all I had ever wanted to hear. I had spent 14 years waiting for her to call my name.

Mummy, I'm home!

Over the next couple of years, I'm hoping to find a patch of land to cultivate and turn into a memorial garden for Charlene – I'd like somewhere my grandkids can play and plant flowers and vegetables and think of her. And it may be too ambitious, but I would like to open a youth centre, too. I'd call it The Charlene Downes Centre. She would love that, seeing her name in lights.

'I'm a celeb,' she'd say, with her trademark cheeky giggle. 'Just like Darren Day!'

And through the centre, I'd like to offer counselling and support. Games of pool and football. Coffee and cakes. Just somewhere for kids, like Charlene, to meet and talk. Because if Charlene had felt able to confide in someone – *anyone* – her life might well have been saved. And if I could rescue one girl, it would be a wonderful legacy for my daughter. It's a pipe dream, but my dream all the same.

And I dream of bringing her home for a respectful burial too. But again, this is just another pipe dream – I probably will never have enough money to find out what happened to my daughter, I won't ever have the resources to bring her body back home. At the time of writing, the funding for the search of Madeleine McCann has now surpassed £11 million, and only recently more money was pledged to the Metropolitan Police to continue with their inquiries. I am used to being marginalised, but it still rankles; it still hurts. If I'm honest, I have no faith left at all in the police. The inquiry into Charlene's death was either a cock-up or a cover-up. Either way, although the investigation is still officially ongoing, I feel justice is further away now than it has ever been.

I would like to make other parents aware of the dangers of child exploitation and grooming. I was totally unaware

– so naive as to what was happening right under my nose. I was so trusting, and so preoccupied with life's little niggles, that I failed to see the evil that would eventually steal her from me. If one family can learn from Charlene's tragedy, it will bring me some comfort and warmth.

Of course, there is the smallest part of me, and I dare not even allow myself to think it, that believes Charlene might still be alive. But I no longer cling feverishly to that desperate hope, because I know it is so destructive. But if she was to read this, I would like her to know, that I have never, and will never, truly give up on holding her in my arms again.

For the present, and that is where I have learned to live now, I focus on my wonderful grandchildren. Emma's youngest, Tallulah, has incredibly long legs, just like her aunty did. And Robert's Maisie is uncannily similar in her nature. She has that same quirky outlook on life, that same infectious little giggle. I can imagine Maisie laughing hysterically if she ever saw the little dog sitting in the pram, just as Charlene did, all those years ago. The two of them tick along in harmony together; they are on the same page of life, even though they are so cruelly separated by two worlds. But those two worlds are not distinct. And a part of Charlene lives on through all of my grandchildren, and that knowledge has helped to heal my heartbreak.

I don't dwell on her death. I want to remember the girl she was, the love she gave and the happiness she brought to us all.

ACKNOWLEDGEMENTS

I would like to thank the following people for all their support: my beloved mum, Emma, Rebecca, Rob Downes (Junior), Bob Downes (Senior), Mr John McNally, Joe and Ann Cusack, Mr Martin Gorton (Gilbert), Mr Mark Clifton, Mr Mark Butcher, Abbey Butcher, SAMM Merseyside (Marie McCourt and John), Terry Watson, and all the members of the Amazing Graze Soup Kitchen for their unconditional love and support.

I would also like to thank Blink Publishing who made this book possible.